T0194982

Conversing With God

Prayer is a Privilege

Jerome N Terry

WESTBOW
P R E S S®
A DIVISION OF THOMAS NELSON
& ZONDERVAN

WestBow Press books may be ordered through booksellers or by contacting:

WestBow Press
A Division of Thomas Nelson & Zondervan
1663 Liberty Drive
Bloomington, IN 47403
www.westbowpress.com
1 (866) 928-1240

ISBN: 978-1-9736-9102-0 (sc)
ISBN: 978-1-9736-9103-7 (hc)
ISBN: 978-1-9736-9101-3 (e)

Library of Congress Control Number: 2020907607

Print information available on the last page.

WestBow Press rev. date: 05/08/2020

This book is dedicated to my parents: Noyd and Lula Mae Terry
My Paternal Grand Parents: Richard and Lucinda Terry
To my Siblings
To my Grand Children and Great Grand Children

I am Blessed By The Best, his name is Jesus
Christ and he has enough for you too!

Foreword

Psalms 6:9 The Lord hath heard my supplication; the Lord will receive my prayer. Amen

When I was asked by the author to write a Foreword for this amazing God-Inspired book of prayers I felt truly blessed. The author Pastor Jerome N. Terry is my brother. I would like to take this time to thank my Big Brother for the opportunity to contribute to his book. Jerome is the oldest of five children born to the union of Noyd and Lula Mae Terry. Our parents were God fearing people who taught us the "Our Father Prayer" as soon as we were able to speak. We were also taught that all struggles are presented to the Lord with prayer and thanksgiving. I remember our parents saying when you trust and believe in God you know your prayers are heard. With that being said Jerome is a man of God whom I love and respect. I believe many hours of fervent prayer went into the development of this book. I am sure the book will be a blessing to all who are privileged to read it. Please allow the Holy Spirit to lead and guide you on your spiritual journey through this wonderful book of prayers and please share with others who are in need.

1 John 5:14-15 And this is the confidence that we have in him, that if we ask anything according to his will, he heareth us and if we know that he hear us, whatsoever we ask, we know that we have the petitions that we desired of him. Amen

Jerome's loving Sister,
Cecile Terry Leavell

Therefore I tell you, whatever you ask for in prayer, believe that you have received it, and it will be yours. **(Mark 11:24 NIV)**

I felt honored when asked to do this Foreword for this awesome prayer book. I truly respect, love and appreciate the author Pastor Jerome N. Terry. You see, he is my Pastor, my friend, my spiritual leader, my prayer support partner but most of all he is My Big Brother. I remember when we were children our parents… especially my mother always told us to stay together as a family and to love each other always. We were taught to hug each other and kiss each other and bond in brotherly and sisterly love which to this day we still do these things. We were taught from children to go to church every Sunday to love the Lord and to pray to God about everything. We had a praying mother and a praying father, and I thank God that was instilled in us from a young age. Now my Big Brother is a Pastor and we are all still members of the church body and we all love the Lord. I am very proud of my Big Brother and his journey. This book is exceptional, it will guide you and direct your daily path to keeping the faith in God and staying on your spiritual journey with God.

Always remember saints of God…Prayer Changes Things

With love always your baby sister,
Toni T. Roman

Prayer is one of the most talked, written and practiced spiritual disciplines for believers. Prayer is our daily way to communicate with a higher power (God) whatever, you perceive Him to be. Paul's command in 1 Thessalonians 5:17 to *"pray without ceasing,"* can be confusing. Obviously, it cannot mean we are to be in a head-bowed, eyes-closed posture all day long. Paul is not referring to non-stop talking, but rather an attitude of God-consciousness and God-surrender that we carry with us all the time.

Prayer makes a difference. Prayer is a two-way communication with God. God is always listening, and he will deliver if you have the faith when you pray.

I have known Jerome N. Terry my entire life. I have witnessed how God has transformed him into a disciple of Christ to deliver God's word to all people. He has experienced many challenges in life. Nonetheless, God still kept him and placed him on the path he has taken this day as a pastoral calling at Bethel Lutheran Church in New Orleans, LA. He is a man of God and has a heart of compassion when he prays. When he prays, he prays for all mankind and sincerely uplifts everyone in prayer asking for God's favor and deliverance. He is a man after God's heart and has prayed to God to create a clean heart in him and renew a right spirit within him. Therefore, when God creates a clean heart in an individual the heart is PURE because it is God's doing.

Like the Apostle Paul, Jerome N. Terry has set out a new way of speaking to individuals by allowing God to speak to him. Through much sacrifice and prayer God has chosen him as a vessel to publish a book on prayer. God has given Jerome N. Terry a vision to write a book on prayer. It is my belief that God is speaking not only to him but through him. Through his teachings and devotions many individuals have accepted Christ as their personal Savior.

Jerome N. Terry's book on prayer will offer you a road map on how to communicate with God. It is my hope that you will join Jerome N. Terry on this venture and devote daily prayer time with God. It's only by the grace of God we are here. Therefore, before you let the devil win, go back and pray again because prayer will change things.

Tyrone K. Terry

Conversing With God

Prayer is a Privilege

Here we will find concise and beautiful prayers as the Gospel message guides us to implore God, by His grace and through His mercy–to establish His love in and through our thoughts, words, and deeds. We pray these things to recall who always provides for us, and to receive these gifts with devout thanksgiving.

In prayer we have an opportunity to deeply and personally connect with God. In your prayer life you should become brutally honest with what you feel, what you say, what you think and what you want. God does not want religious clichés; He wants your honest bared heart as you speak with Him.

As we approach God's throne of grace, let us remember to say to him:

We pray through Jesus Christ, your Son, our Lord,
and redeemer, who lives and reigns with you and the
Holy Spirit, one God, now and forever. Amen

1

The LORD is slow to anger and great in power; the LORD will not leave the guilty unpunished. His way is in the whirlwind and the storm, and clouds are the dust of his feet. (Nahum 1:3 NIV)

LORD God Awesome and Mighty in Power and Compassion, LORD you are slow to anger and long suffering with your created people. Yet O God we know from your word that the guilty will stand in judgment before your throne at the resurrection. LORD, have mercy for the sake of the bitter innocent suffering and death of Jesus Christ our Savior. LORD, renew our hearts, minds, and actions to coincide with your will while we are still on earth. In Jesus's name we pray. Amen

**And we know that all things work together for good
to those who love God, to those who are the called
according to His purpose. (Romans 8:28 NKJV)**

Father God in Heaven, we do not understand the how or why, you allow suffering and pain in this life. LORD in our ignorance we often question your seemingly blind nonobservance of tragedy, disaster, injustice, and wickedness in this world. We know you do not take pleasure in our pain. We know your word says that even during suffering you can reveal your good will in our lives. We trust you LORD because out of what seems to be the greatest evil, you alone O God can produce the greatest good. Thank you for Christ Jesus who suffered the evil of the cross which produced the greatest good for all of mankind. Amen

3

**For therein is the righteousness of God revealed
from faith to faith: as it is written, The just shall
live by faith.(Romans 1:17 KJV)**

O God our Father in Heaven, we children of men are often challenged by assignments which are ordained by you. Father God because we lack the necessary faith in you, we shrink away from the challenge saying, "I can't do that". Father strengthen our faith for it is written: "The righteous shall live by faith". Lord, increase our faith we ask in Jesus's name. Amen

4

**For the eyes of the Lord are over the righteous,
and his ears are open unto their prayers: but
the face of the Lord is against them that do evil.
(1 Peter 3:12 KJV)**

Lord of Righteousness, we ask your forgiveness for falling short as we sin in thought, word, and deed. Thank you, Father God for sending Christ Jesus who is our righteousness. Because of Christ Jesus, your eyes view us as righteous and you continually open your ears to our prayers. Help us O God to live up to the decency showered on us through Christ Jesus. Amen

5

But I say unto you, Love your enemies, bless them that curse you, do good to them that hate you, and pray for them which despitefully use you, and persecute you; (Matthew 5:44 KJV)

Lord God Almighty, there are people who speak evil against us. Lord there are people who seek to harm us either physically, financially, relationally or mentally. Father God these people consider us as enemies. Help us to pray for them O God. Help us to bless them O God. Help us to not return evil for evil. Father God in the name of Jesus help us to not speak an ill word against another human being. Amen

6

Give thanks to the LORD, call on his name; make known among the nations what he has done. (Psalm 105:1 NIV)

LORD God who does wonders, we see daily your modern-day miracles of healing, restoration, reconciliation and repentant hearts seeking salvation. Lord help us all who are the recipients of your inspired great deeds in our lives to share this good news with those who have not experienced you through such works. In Jesus's name we pray. Amen

7

Finally, all of you, live in harmony with one another; be sympathetic, love as brothers, be compassionate and humble. (1 Peter 3:8 NIV)

Our God who is Love, hear us as we pray in the name of Jesus. Father God touch our hearts that we may live in harmony with each other. LORD God let us be sympathetic towards the condition of one another. Father God help us to love as you have loved us and to do so in humility. Almighty Father, this we ask in Jesus's name. Amen

8

Who endowed the heart with wisdom or gave understanding to the mind? (Job 38:36 NIV)

Ancient of Days, who is like you? You store the lightening. You tell the sea come this far and no farther. And LORD you endow the hearts of your people with wisdom. Father God you give understanding to the mind. What an awesome and Mighty God you are. Thank you, LORD, for caring for us in our human frailty; we are weak, but you are strong. In Jesus's name we praise and worship you. Amen

9

For as often as you eat this bread and drink the cup, you proclaim the Lord's death until he comes. (1 Corinthians 11:26 NIV)

Lord Jesus, Maundy Thursday is recognized as the traditional day of the first Lord's Supper. Lord as we partake of the sacrament of the Alter or share a Seder meal in remembrance of this day; let your people remember the awesome sacrifice you made for our forgiveness, so that no more will our sins be remembered. Thank you, Lord Jesus for bringing us back into relationship with the Father. Amen

10

Then the man said, "Let me go, for it is daybreak." But Jacob replied, "I will not let you go unless you bless me." (Genesis 32:26 NIV)

Ever Present and Eternal Father God, we like Jacob say to you, "I will not let you go unless you bless me." Even after your blessing Father God we do not desire you to leave our presence. Father God bless our church, home, nation, health, finances, relationships, spiritual wellbeing, families, and friends. Father God your promise is that you will never leave us. For this and the love expressed to us through Christ Jesus we praise and thank you. In Jesus's name we pray. Amen

11

I want to know Christ and the power of his resurrection and the fellowship of sharing in his sufferings, becoming like him in his death. (Philippians 3:10 NIV)

O Lord Jesus our Suffering Savior, we eagerly await the day when we will see you face to face and ask once again a final request for forgiveness. Lord how can we not ask over and over for forgiveness, because of you taking our deserved punishment upon yourself. Lord we cannot thank, praise, or ask for mercy enough to satisfy the debt we owe. Lord in your mercy, hear our prayer. Amen

12

Greater love has no one than this, that he lay down his life for his friends. (John 15:13 NIV)

Lord God of Love, we your hand made children often profess love but that has strings attached. Lord we love because of, but you O God love in spite of. LORD thank you for the love sent through our Savior Jesus who died in our stead. In Jesus's name we pray. Amen

13

Do not let any unwholesome talk come out of your mouths, but only what is helpful for building others up according to their needs, that it may benefit those who listen. (Ephesians 4:29 NIV)

LORD God Heavenly Father, we children of men speak negatively of your creation and of one another. LORD, forgive us for speaking against your creation. LORD, help us to speak life into the lives of each other. Father God, this we ask in Jesus's name. Amen

14

Is anything too hard for the LORD? At the appointed time I will return to you, about this time next year, and Sarah shall have a son." (Genesis 18:14 ESV)

Lord God, you accomplish your purposes; there is nothing too hard for you. Our hope is in you alone. Although we try to fix our problems, the result is found in your hands. LORD you can do anything but fail. In Jesus's name help us to trust you and in that, wholly. In Jesus's name we pray. Amen

15

Be perfect, therefore, as your heavenly Father is perfect. (Matthew 5:48 NIV)

Most Gracious Heavenly Father God, you are the Almighty and there is none like you. Father God, perfect us–your imperfect people–to be more like you in thought, word, and deed. Father God make us more Christ like in every way; this is our desire. This we ask in Jesus's name. Amen

16

At one time we too were foolish, disobedient, deceived and enslaved by all kinds of passions and pleasures. We lived in malice and envy, being hated and hating one another. (Titus 3:3 NIV)

Dear Father God, we your children change in appearance, maturity, and spirituality. Thank you–LORD for working change in our lives as we met Jesus. Thank you–LORD for the touch of Jesus, changing us from what we were to what you want us to be. In Jesus's name we pray. Amen

17

Trust in him at all times, O people; pour out your heart before him; God is a refuge for us. Selah (Psalm 62:8 ESV)

LORD God Almighty, in the name of Jesus we declare you alone are our refuge. We find comfort LORD God when we relinquish self-control and seek Godly control. Thank you, LORD God, for being stronger than any difficulty we face in this life. Father God hear our prayer in Jesus's name. Amen

18

Oh, taste and see that the LORD *is* good; Blessed *is* the man *who* trusts in Him! (Psalm 34:8 NKJV)

LORD God Our Heavenly Father, when we try to go it alone, we fail every time. LORD your protection from the enemy is impregnable and blessed are those who seek you as their sanctuary. Thank you for being our safe–haven. LORD in your mercy and by the name of Jesus, hear our prayer. Amen

19

Let the word of Christ dwell in you richly as you teach and admonish one another with all wisdom, and as you sing psalms, hymns and spiritual songs with gratitude in your hearts to God. (Colossians 3:16 NIV)

Gracious and Loving Father God–house the Word of Christ Jesus in our hearts that we may teach one another with prudence as we observe opportunity to do so. In aiding one another LORD let us do so with psalms, hymns, and thankful hearts as we express love one to another. In Jesus's name we pray. Amen

20

Now this is the confidence that we have in Him, that if we ask anything according to His will, He hears us. (1 John 5:14 NKJV)

Most High God our Rock and our Redeemer, we come to you asking forgiveness for past sins and help in not repeating those mistakes again. We come confidently knowing that as we ask anything in your will, you hear us and act according to your great will. LORD, hear our prayer, in Jesus's name we ask this. Amen

21

You will seek me and find me when you seek me with all your heart. (Jeremiah 29:13 NIV)

O LORD our God who pursue His lost sheep, People often say I found the Lord, but Lord God the truth is you were never lost. We are the lost and as we seek you it is only when we do so with our whole hearts that we then find you. LORD the amazing thing is that as we meet you, we find that you have continually pursued us, even in our ignorance. We thank you LORD for seeking that which was lost, in the name of Jesus we pray. Amen

22

Beloved, let us love one another, for love is of God; and everyone who loves is born of God and knows God. (1 John 4:7 NKJV)

Father God our Creator, you manifested your love in creating this world and all its provisions for your ultimate creation, mankind. Thank you, LORD God. Inspire us to take better care of your created world so that those who come behind us can enjoy the natural beauty, wildlife, resources, and habitation you have for your hand made servants. Father God–help us to love one another by saving the planet for future generations until the coming of Christ our Lord and Savior. In Jesus's name we pray. Amen

23

And do not be conformed to this world, but be transformed by the renewing of your mind, that you may prove what *is* that good and acceptable and perfect will of God. (Romans 12:2 NKJV)

Dear Heavenly Father God of change, we your handmade servants try to get life right by consciously monitoring our actions. Father God, no matter how hard we try we fail. LORD, renew our minds and cleanse our hearts as we come seeking forgiveness for our sin. Father God, in Jesus's name we ask that you change us from what we are to what you want us to be. Help us Lord to walk in your word. In Jesus's name we pray. Amen

24

For this my son was dead, and is alive again; he was lost, and is found. And they began to be merry. (Luke 15:24 KJV)

LORD God Almighty Father of mercy, thank you that you are not like man. Father when we stray and return with a repentant heart you do not lecture and reprimand you only lovingly open your arms and say welcome home my child. Father God help those who profess your love to do likewise towards those who lose their way and later return. Lord, hear our prayer in Jesus's name. Amen

25

O God, You *are* my God; Early will I seek You; My soul thirsts for You; My flesh longs for You In a dry and thirsty land Where there is no water. (Psalm 63:1 NKJV)

LORD God our Heavenly Father, we approach you early each morning in the name of Jesus, seeking your divine guidance as we begin our day. Help us to honestly share our failures, hopes, disappointments and dreams with you daily so we may build a lasting intimate love relationship with you–through Christ our Savior. Help us O God to hear as you speak into our lives–giving guidance, mercy, care, and love. Lord, hear our prayers in Jesus's name. Amen

26

I will praise you as long as I live, and in your name I will lift up my hands. (Psalm 63:4 NIV)

Father God the Great IAM, You O God are all that we will ever need in this life and eternity to come. Thank you, LORD for loving us even with our sinful shortcomings. LORD in the name of Jesus we lift our voices, hearts, and hands to you in praise because you are worthy to be praised. LORD, hear our prayer in the name of Jesus. Amen

When pride comes, then comes disgrace, but with humility comes wisdom. (Proverbs 11:2 NIV)

Almighty and Eternal Father God hear us as we pray in the name of Jesus. LORD, keep us from the false hope which pride brings. Father let us not become disgraced by our inward reflection and lack of reliance on you as the one on whom we place our focus. LORD, keep us humble and grant us wisdom. This we ask in Jesus's name. Amen

28

"And it shall come to pass afterward That I will pour out My Spirit on all flesh; Your sons and your daughters shall prophesy, Your old men shall dream dreams, Your young men shall see visions. (Joel 2:28 NKJV)

Omnipotent God our Father, your spirit is poured out upon all flesh for the sanctification of mankind. LORD, help your children to rededicate their lives to you daily that we may honor you by our thoughts, words, and deed. Lord in Jesus's name we pray. Amen

29

Therefore, my beloved brothers, be steadfast, immovable, always abounding in the work of the Lord, knowing that in the Lord your labor is not in vain. (1 Corinthians 15:58 ESV)

O Lord our God and Savior help us live for you each day. Empower us O God to follow you in what you are doing, so that we walk in your will and not self-will. In Jesus's name we pray. Amen

30

Give us this day our daily bread. (Matthew 6:11 NKJV)

LORD God you are our Jehovah-Jireh, Father God your daily provision of our needs gives us joy and make us whole. Help us to understand and faithfully accept your daily provision as we with joyful hearts use what you have given for self and others. In Jesus's name we pray. Amen

31

Let the word of Christ dwell in you richly in all wisdom, teaching and admonishing one another in psalms and hymns and spiritual songs, singing with grace in your hearts to the Lord. (Colossians 3:16 NKJV)

Almighty and Everlasting Father God our LORD, forgive us when we doubt you by questioning your word. Help us to be sensitive to your work in our lives through the continued blessings you bestow. Father let your word become alive in us as we teach and correct one another regarding you and how you operate in the lives of your children. Father God we exalt your name with song, prayer, praise, worship and with thankful hearts. In Jesus's name we pray. Amen

32

In that day you will no longer ask me anything. I tell you the truth, my Father will give you whatever you ask in my name. (John 16:23 NIV)

Lord Jesus, we come boldly but humbly asking that you speak peace into our lives as we walk yet on this side of eternity. Lord there are many conflicts in this world. People are divided by lust, greed, hatred, and jealousy. Lord during the struggle; help us to forgive those who attempt to use and abuse because they know not what they do. This we ask in the name of the Father, Son and Holy Spirit. Amen

33

And God is able to make all grace abound to you, so that in all things at all times, having all that you need, you will abound in every good work. (2 Corinthians 9:8 NIV)

LORD God Almighty, through Christ Jesus you have made all grace flourish in us thank you. LORD, all we need comes from you and through you. Help us to become abundant in good works for the benefit of one another. This we pray in Jesus's Holy name. Amen

34

Thanks be to God for his indescribable gift! (2 Corinthians 9:15 NIV)

Heavenly Father God, who is there like you? You created us and we fell into sin. You lifted us up and we turned our backs to you. You came as one of us to redeem us by the shedding of your blood, yet mankind still does not get it. You O Lord have given an indescribable gift through your long suffering and patience with mankind. Thank you, O God, for not giving us what we deserve. You forgive us. Thank you for Jesus standing in the gap for us and reconciling us to you. In Jesus's name we pray. Amen

35

Study to shew thyself approved unto God, a workman that needeth not to be ashamed, rightly dividing the word of truth. (2 Timothy 2:15 KJV)

O LORD our God, we children of men often read your word with only minimal comprehension. In these cases, we move on to the next text without the full understanding of the previous text. Lord Jesus, help us to absorb the text, commit the text to our hearts and then live out the text as your true disciples. Lord in your mercy, hear our prayer. Amen

36

The LORD your God is with you, he is mighty to save. He will take great delight in you, he will quiet you with his love, he will rejoice over you with singing." (Zephaniah 3:17 NIV)

O Lord our God, mighty in power yet gentle in dealing with your beloved children. Thank you, Father God, for delighting in us your hand made servants. LORD when life causes us to quake in its onslaught your love gives us tranquility. LORD we rejoice knowing that the love of Jesus Christ our Savior carries us through the toughest of times and situations. Amen

37

Do not neglect your gift, which was given you through a prophetic message when the body of elders laid their hands on you. (1 Timothy 4:14 NIV)

O Lord our God we each have been given gifts of the Spirit. Lord, help us to develop the initial seeding of the gift; allowing it to come to full blossom in our lives–so that others may benefit from the increase. This we pray in the matchless name of Jesus. Amen

38

And on the seventh day God ended His work which He had done, and He rested on the seventh day from all His work which He had done. (Genesis 2:2 NKJV)

We thank you Lord in Jesus's name for strengthening us through a peaceful rest. Help us to follow your lead as you rested from your work. Help us Father, to rest from work, not to just work from rest. In Jesus's name we pray. Amen

39

This is what the LORD says: "Stand at the crossroads and look; ask for the ancient paths, ask where the good way is, and walk in it, and you will find rest for your souls. But you said, 'We will not walk in it.' (Jeremiah 6:16 NIV)

O LORD our God, many times in life we come to an inflection point where we must decide our path towards further progress. Lord, if we go in the wrong direction then we face disastrous results. If we go in the correct direction, then we reap a triumphant benefit. Father God, in the name of Jesus we ask that you direct us in the proper path to take. Lord, show us where the good way is located. This we ask in Jesus's name. Amen

40

And it will be said: "Build up, build up, prepare the road! Remove the obstacles out of the way of my people." (Isaiah 57:14 NIV)

O God you alone are High and Lofty. LORD we build on the road to eternity by placing our faith in Christ Jesus alone. LORD we are developing a relationship with Him as we come to you through Him. Father help us to overcome the stumbling blocks placed in our path set to hinder our progress. In Jesus's name we pray. Amen

41

Make sure that nobody pays back wrong for wrong, but always try to be kind to each other and to everyone else. (1 Thessalonians 5:15 NIV)

Father God of Harmony, many times there are those among us who do us evil regardless of your word. Help us Father God to not return evil for evil. LORD, enable us through Christ Jesus to do good towards everyone, because through Christ we can, and without him we cannot. This we ask in Jesus's name. Amen

42

For he has rescued us from the dominion of darkness and brought us into the kingdom of the Son he loves, (Colossians 1:13 NIV)

Lord God our Redeemer, how can we thank you for the love shown us through the rescue from darkness of this world we live in. LORD, because of your benevolence you have brought us into the kingdom of light by your beloved son Christ Jesus. Thank you, God our Father through our Savior King Jesus. Amen

43

Love does no harm to its neighbor. Therefore, love is the fulfillment of the law. (Romans 13:10 NIV)

LORD God, Essence of Love, too often people hurt one another deliberately. There are times LORD when self-will seeks to injure another. LORD, forgive us for our misguided intentions. LORD God, by the power of your Holy Spirit help us to fulfill the law by offering one another love, not harm. LORD, hear our prayer in Jesus's name. Amen

44

For by him all things were created: things in heaven and on earth, visible and invisible, whether thrones or powers or rulers or authorities; all things were created by him and for him. (Colossians 1:16 NIV)

Lord Jesus, how can the world question your divinity? Scripture speaks to us from Genesis to Revelation; it is all concerning you. In awe, O Lord we see how you created the Heavens and the Earth and the fullness therein. Lord, we see how all of this was created for, and by you. Then for your crowning creation you offered your human life, shedding your precious blood to redeem that which was lost. How great you are, Our Lord, Our Savior, Our God. Amen

45

He who gets wisdom loves his own soul; he who cherishes understanding prospers. (Proverbs 19:8 NIV)

O God our Heavenly Father, we children of men have been given your Spirit of wisdom as a guide through life. Sometimes we follow Him and sometimes we operate in self-directed activity, forgive us our folly. Help us Father God, to understand and be sensitive to the Holy Spirit's teachings. This we ask in Jesus's name. Amen

46

In vain you rise early and stay up late, toiling for food to eat-for he grants sleep to those he loves. (Psalm 127:2 NIV)

Lord God Heavenly Father, thank you for peaceful, restful, healing sleep. Lord we cannot accomplish anything of value when exhausted from the toils of life. Father we work from the rest you give as we work towards achieving a good harvest for you. In Jesus's name we pray. Amen

47

Jesus said to them, "My Father is always at his work to this very day, and I, too, am working." (John 5:17 NIV)

Father God our Creator, we see you at work in our lives and our communities. LORD, empower us to join you in the work we see you doing. Father God, scripture teaches us that the harvest is plentiful, but the workers are few. LORD, help us to become willing workers in the kingdom. In Jesus's precious name we pray. Amen

48

The Lord says: "These people come near to me with their mouth and honor me with their lips, but their hearts are far from me. Their worship of me is made up only of rules taught by men. (Isaiah 29:13 NIV)

O LORD Our God let our mouth's honor you and our hearts be turned to you in true and pure worship. Forgive us where we fell short in the past as we followed man made concepts. Help us LORD God Almighty, by the power of your Holy Spirit to worship you in spirit and truth. This we ask in the name of the Father, Son and Holy Spirit. Amen

49

You yourselves are our letter, written on our hearts, known and read by everybody. (2 Corinthians 3:2 NIV)

LORD God Mighty and Gracious, many people will never cross the threshold of the doors of a church. LORD many will never peel open the pages of the Holy Bible. But LORD many will meet those who profess to be Christian. Help our Lives O God to be such as they leave a positive impression on those we meet. LORD God let our lives be a living, loving Gospel testimony which draws people to Christ. Grant O God, that we not become a stumbling block to someone seeking Christ. Help our life's interaction plant seeds which blossom into a hunger for Christ and not seeds which produce repulsive thorns, thistles, and weeds. LORD hear our prayer in Jesus's name we pray. Amen

50

Do not let any unwholesome talk come out of your mouths, but only what is helpful for building others up according to their needs, that it may benefit those who listen. (Ephesians 4:29 NIV)

O God our Father in Heaven, we children of men often open our mouths in haste. Father God when we speak without thinking we unwittingly harm people around us. Lord God help us to guard our speech that it may always be congenial and edifying. This we pray in Jesus's name. Amen

51

The sacrifices of God are a broken spirit; a broken and contrite heart, O God, you will not despise. (Psalm 51:17 NIV)

Father God Almighty, we come in the name of Jesus asking forgiveness. Often–we think we have life all figured out. LORD we need you, we cannot proceed without you. LORD God, our best efforts end in disaster when we take you out of the equation. LORD, there are many who operate in self-indulgence, protect us from falling prey to that mentality. Holy Spirit prick our hearts that they are broken by misdeeds. O God relieve us of a prideful spirit. LORD, have mercy on us. This we ask in Jesus's name. Amen

52

For we are God's workmanship, created in Christ Jesus to do good works, which God prepared in advance for us to do. (Ephesians 2:10 NIV)

LORD God of hosts, we are crafted in your image, created in Christ Jesus to do good works. Help us to always function in this manner while we are yet on this side of the cross. And Father as we accomplish those good works help us not revel in those works as if they lead to Salvation. Help us LORD to understand we do works as a remembrance of your love, mercy, and grace towards us. This we pray in Jesus's name. Amen

53

"Remember the Sabbath day by keeping it holy. (Exodus 20:8 NIV)

Lord God Almighty, thank you for reminding us of the importance of maintaining a Sabbath day. Father we keep the Sabbath as a day of worship and rest. Help us O God to always practice keeping a Sabbath day which we hold Holy and special to you. In Jesus's name we pray. Amen

54

The LORD is near to all who call on him, to all who call on him in truth. (Psalm 145:18 NIV)

Gracious Father God, you are near those who call on you. LORD you always answer those who believe on you and seek you with faith. LORD we believe that you exist and you through Christ Jesus are the object of our faith. Thank you for being there for us no matter what day or hour. We are unworthy of your consideration, but then, you are the one and only Gracious Father God, full of love and compassion. Hear us O God in Jesus's name. Amen

55

"Come, all you who are thirsty, come to the waters; and you who have no money, come, buy and eat! Come, buy wine and milk without money and without cost. (Isaiah 55:1 NIV)

O Lord our God who provides, Father you summon us to the banquet of salvation which is administered through the Lamb who is without blemish or defect. LORD you tell us to come and receive of the life-giving water you have provided. O God you say come and partake of the bread of life at no cost. Father God how can we not thank you for the abundant free, gift of life you have so graciously provided to us. We are a people who despite your gracious love often reject you as we sin in thought, word, and deed. Forgive us Lord for our error. This we pray in the name of Jesus. Amen

56

your eyes saw my unformed body. All the days ordained for me were written in your book before one of them came to be. (Psalm 139:16 NIV)

Lord God, before we were molded into human form you knew us. Lord even the days of our lives are prerecorded in your book of life. Thank you for knowing us before human eyes viewed us. Thank you for loving us from beginning to the end of our days. Thank you for knowing us better than we know ourselves. Thank you for Jesus's saving grace. This we pray in Jesus's name. Amen

57

I know that nothing good lives in me, that is, in my sinful nature. For I have the desire to do what is good, but I cannot carry it out. (Romans 7:18 NIV)

Merciful Father God, daily we struggle with the choice of our actions leading us to the right or the left. Some things Lord we knowingly do which are outside of your will for us. Father at other times we slip into sinful action before we are aware that it has us in its grip. Lord, sin is ever in us, ever present, ever seeking to display itself in reality–through us. Lord God–help us to not yield to sins seductive enticement. Father God cover us with the blood of Christ Jesus that sin may not get through to us leading us astray. This we pray in Jesus's name. Amen

58

He will sit as a refiner and purifier of silver; he will purify the Levites and refine them like gold and silver. Then the LORD will have men who will bring offerings in righteousness. (Malachi 3:3 NIV)

O God, refine us, purify us as a refiner purifies gold. O God remove all impurification and toss the dross into the abyss from which it came. O Father direct our spiritual life as we relinquish the debris in our lives as you burn away the distractions, burn away the junk, burn away the disobedience which has been collected throughout our lives. O God create in us a clean heart that we may serve you and not self. This we pray in Jesus's name. Amen.

59

Since the children have flesh and blood, he too shared in their humanity so that by his death he might destroy him who holds the power of death-- that is, the devil. (Hebrews 2:14 NIV)

Lord Jesus, you came clothed as we are in human flesh, that you through that action might experience and share our human condition. Lord, you accomplished what no other human could do. You, O Lamb of God–defeated him who holds the power over death, that we whom you created may no longer fear death but look forward to eternal life. Lord Jesus, in your mercy, hear our prayer. Amen

60

Though he brings grief, he will show compassion, so great is his unfailing love. (Lamentations 3:32 NIV)

Lord God our Redeemer, you judge mankind and you restore mankind. LORD there is no love greater than the love you display towards your people. Thank you, LORD, for your unfailing mercy. Hear our prayer in Jesus's name, as we pray. Amen

61

Those who know your name will trust in you, for you, LORD, have never forsaken those who seek you. (Psalm 9:10 NIV)

O LORD our God, people must know you in order to trust you. Thank you, LORD that you have made your name known to us. As we continue to seek you LORD while we are yet on this side of the cross, help us to share our knowledge of your name and love with those we meet. O LORD you have never forsaken those who seek you. You are the awesome and loving God. LORD in your mercy, hear our prayer. Amen

62

He who conceals his sins does not prosper, but whoever confesses and renounces them finds mercy. (Proverbs 28:13 NIV)

O God our Father, sin is sin. Very often we seek to minimize the sin that so easily trips us up. Help us to not attempt to hide the sin we are immersed in. Help us Lord to draw on the power of the Holy Spirit to confess and renounce the sin we find ourselves sinking in. Lord, have mercy on us. This we ask in Jesus's name. Amen

63

The bed is too short to stretch out on, the blanket too narrow to wrap around you. (Isaiah 28:20 NIV)

Father God in Heaven, we children of men try to create our own rest through our own actions. Father God forgive us; remind us never will we find rest until it comes from you through Christ Jesus. In Jesus's name we pray. Amen

64

Save me, O LORD, from lying lips and from deceitful tongues. (Psalm 120:2 NIV)

O LORD God Almighty, we children of men deceive, manipulate, exaggerate, falsely flatter, and excuse our shortcomings using lies. LORD we lie in what we say and what we do not say. Your Word O LORD says" No one who practices deceit will dwell in My House". LORD, help us, forgive us, and empower us to avoid deceit, either practiced or perceived. This we pray in Jesus's name. Amen

65

You are the light of the world. A city that is set on a hill cannot be hidden. (Matthew 5:14 NKJV)

Lord God, Heavenly Father, help your handmade servants to share the light of the Gospel in this world. Father God let the light of Jesus Christ eradicate the darkness of sin because light casts out all darkness. In Jesus's name, the Light of the World we pray. Amen

66

And that is what some of you were. But you were washed, you were sanctified, you were justified in the name of the Lord Jesus Christ and by the Spirit of our God. (1 Corinthians 6:11 NIV)

Father of Mercies, we your handmade servants are sinful by nature. Father God we cannot rid ourselves of the sin which clings to us.

Father God in the name of Jesus we thank you for the washing in the blood of Jesus which sanctify us. Thank you, LORD God Almighty that we are justified by faith in the name of the Lord Jesus Christ and empowered by your Holy Spirit. In Jesus's name we pray. Amen

67

"But blessed is the man who trusts in the LORD, whose confidence is in him. (Jeremiah 17:7 NIV)

LORD God of Peace–help us to keep our trust in you alone and not in men who falter and fail. Help us O God to not despair in times of doubt but to look to you in confidence; that you will bless and impart favor in every situation in our lives according to your will. Help us to live this in all matters in life. In Jesus's name we pray. Amen

68

Wait for the LORD; be strong and take heart and wait for the LORD. (Psalm 27:14 NIV)

LORD God Strong and Mighty, give our faint hearts the necessary courage to wait on you our Faithful God. Strengthen us O God in our human weakness. Forgive us as we have walked in lax reliance on you. This we pray in Jesus's name. Amen

69

The LORD replied, "My Presence will go with you, and I will give you rest." (Exodus 33:14 NIV)

Most High God, we know you are always with us as we go through this life. Thank you, LORD. In knowing that you are ever with us we can rest from the cares of this world. We thank you in Jesus's name. Amen

70

Be joyful in hope, patient in affliction, faithful in prayer. (Romans 12:12 NIV)

LORD God who hears our Prayers, we your hand made servants are joyful for the hope we have through Christ Jesus. Father God let our hope spill over into our daily lives as we go through the trials and tribulations of life. Loving Master help us to be faithful in prayer to you as our faith and hope increases in Christ Jesus our Savior. In Jesus's name we pray. Amen

71

Be devoted to one another in brotherly love. Honor one another above yourselves. (Romans 12:10 NIV)

Father God our Creator, we are all a part of your family and as such we should honor one another as your children–created in your image. Forgive us LORD for not doing so. Renew our mind through your Holy Spirit that we may be able to esteem others above ourselves. This we pray in the name of the Father, Son and Holy Spirit. Amen

72

If a man makes a vow to the LORD, or swears an oath to bind himself by some agreement, he shall not break his word; he shall do according to all that proceeds out of his mouth. (Numbers 30:2 NKJV)

LORD you are the truth, we children of men often fall short of the truth. We tint our dialogue with varied phrases which are gray and not definitive in shedding accuracy on our conversations. LORD, help us to speak our words with honesty and let us be bound by the words of our mouths; help us to keep our word. We pray this in the name of the Father, Son and Holy Spirit. Amen

73

You will be blessed when you come in and blessed when you go out. (Deuteronomy 28:6 NIV)

LORD God of Love, you bless us as we go; you bless us as we come, thank you for your continued undeserved blessing. In Jesus's name we pray. Amen

74

Understanding is a fountain of life to those who have it, but folly brings punishment to fools. (Proverbs 16:22 NIV)

LORD God of Compassion, touch those of us who have no understanding, those who act foolishly and those who reject sound instruction. Father God, regardless of their ignorance shield those who think themselves wise yet act foolhardy. LORD in your Mercy and in the name of Jesus, hear our Prayer. Amen

75

Praise the LORD, O my soul, and forget not all his benefits who forgives all your sins and heals all your diseases, (Psalm 103:2-3 NIV)

Father God of Comfort and Mercy, LORD God we are called to praise for the many blessings you give daily. LORD, forgive us if ever we should forget all your blessed benefits. We thank you LORD, as you–through Christ Jesus forgive us our sins, heal us of infirmity and save us from eternal death. In Jesus's name we pray. Amen

76

After the earthquake came a fire, but the LORD was not in the fire. And after the fire came a gentle whisper. (1 Kings 19:12 NIV)

LORD God of Power and Might, you inhabit the fierce elements of nature, yet you are a gentle God who comforts his precious people. Help us O God to seek you in the quietness. Help us O God to have the confidence of knowing that you are ever present and because of that we can rest from the cares of this world. Give us the same strength and resolve which enabled Christ Jesus to walk to the cross of Calvary. We ask that we may be found worthy of the name Christian by which we identify ourselves. LORD, hear our Prayer in Jesus's name. Amen

77

Who are you to judge someone else's servant? To his own master he stands or falls. And he will stand, for the Lord is able to make him stand. (Romans 14:4 NIV)

Lord God of the Harvest, we children of men often stand in judgment concerning another man's theology. Lord we are not divine, we did not create the universe and all that is in it, you did. Lord God, you judge mankind not us. Lord, help us to understand that we do not need to defend nor clarify our theological positions to another human being. Lord, help us to defend only that Christ Jesus died for our sins and through him we are made righteous in your sight. Lord, hear our prayer in Jesus's name. Amen

78

No temptation has seized you except what is common to man. And God is faithful; he will not let you be tempted beyond what you can bear.

But when you are tempted, he will also provide a way out so that you can stand up under it. (1 Corinthians 10:13 NIV)

LORD God our Creator, you who lives forever, as we your handmade servants' walk through this life we are lured by many enticements. LORD, the expectations and desires that are placed before us for our utilization can sometimes drag us into the act of deifying corruption. LORD God, in your mercy forgive us for glorifying our selfish lusts as something supreme. LORD, empower us when we call on the name of Jesus to relieve us of temptation and show us the path past it. Because Christ himself suffered when he was tempted, he alone is our guide. Lord in your Mercy hear our Prayer. Amen

79

Every good and perfect gift is from above, coming down from the Father of the heavenly lights, who does not change like shifting shadows. (James 1:17 NIV)

LORD God the giver of every good and perfect gift. Father God you have opened your hand from above to give us life. Most of all Father God you give us undeserved love and that love manifested itself in the man named Jesus. Thank you, LORD for sending Jesus, then allowing us to ask forgiveness of our sins in his name. Thank you, LORD for never turning your back on us and for the Lamb of God who takes away our sins making us righteous in your sight. We pray in Jesus's name. Amen

80

Whether you turn to the right or to the left, your ears will hear a voice behind you, saying, "This is the way; walk in it." (Isaiah 30:21 NIV)

Gracious and Holy Lord God, you are there to give direction to those of your people who are inclined to hear you speak into their lives. Lord God, we can trust you to guide us in the right path as we go through life. Help us O God to be sensitive to hearing you speak into our lives as you say this is the way to go. This we pray in Jesus's name. Amen

81

And a highway will be there; it will be called the Way of Holiness. The unclean will not journey on it; it will be for those who walk in that Way; wicked fools will not go about on it. (Isaiah 35:8 NIV)

Most Holy LORD and God, you have set apart a road for the redeemed a road which is the Way of Holiness. LORD on this processional highway will be all who have called on the name of Jesus seeking forgiveness and His grace. LORD even the fool can travel this road if he turns back to you and reject the ways of the world. Thank you, LORD, for all you have done, are doing and will do. In Jesus's name we pray, Amen

82

For the sake of his great name the LORD will not reject his people, because the LORD was pleased to make you his own. (1 Samuel 12:22 NIV)

O LORD Our God whose name is IAM, because of your name you will not reject your people is spite of our sinful nature. Thank you, LORD for not turning away in disgust but instead opening your loving arms; calling us to come to you. Thank you that through Christ Jesus you have made us your own. In Jesus's name we pray. Amen

83

But I tell you that men will have to give account on the day of judgment for every careless word they have spoken. (Matthew 12:36 NIV)

Almighty and Everlasting Father God, we children of men speak unhealthy damaging words into the lives of each other. Lord as a knife cuts so too do our words hack away at those; we mean to harm using our conversation. Lord, help us to guard our words because we will one day be judged for every harmful word ever spoken from our mouths. Lord by Jesus's Holy name keep our lips from unwholesome talk. Amen

84

He said to them, "Go into all the world and preach the good news to all creation. (Mark 16:15 NIV)

Heavenly Father, Thank you for another day. Thank you for another opportunity to witness to the lost. Thank you for another opportunity to be better today than yesterday. Help us live this day to your glory. Through Christ Jesus we ask this. Amen

85

But if we walk in the light, as he is in the light, we have fellowship with one another, and the blood of Jesus, his Son, purifies us from all sin. (1 John 1:7 NIV)

Lord God, who purifies and heals, help us to walk in the light of Christ Jesus which casts out all darkness that we may have fellowship with you and one another. In Jesus's name we pray. Amen

86

And over all these virtues put on love, which binds them all together in perfect unity. (Colossians 3:14 NIV)

LORD God Almighty, you are love. Father God, you are the love which binds all things together in perfect harmony. We children of men profess love, but we love with conditions attached. Help us O God to love with the perfection of true love. Father God, you demonstrated this through Christ Jesus who loved us to the point of offering his life, that we through his love would be set free from sin and condemnation. In Jesus's Holy name we pray. Amen

87

Examine yourselves to see whether you are in the faith; test yourselves. Do you not realize that Christ Jesus is in you--unless, of course, you fail the test? (2 Corinthians 13:5 NIV)

Lord Jesus, we know you are in us, but we do not always live as you desire us to. Lord, because of who you are we can honestly test ourselves with impunity. Although we have freedom from punishment through you Lord, our faith walk requires constant self-assessment, repentance, and honesty with who we really are, and the sinful nature which seeks to drag us down into the world. Lord, have mercy on us and help us. Lord, investigate our hearts and if you should find anything unpleasing to you please remove it and fill that void with your Holy Spirit. This we pray in the name of the Father, Son and Holy Spirit. Amen

88

And he passed in front of Moses, proclaiming, "The LORD, the LORD, the compassionate and gracious God, slow to anger, abounding in love and faithfulness, (Exodus 34:6 NIV)

LORD God of Compassion and Grace, your consideration of us poor sinful beings are a mystery to our carnal minds. LORD in many cases we do not show mercy to one another and hold each other to the highest accountability. But you the creator of all things display grace and compassion despite our willful participation in sin. Thank you, LORD, for not giving us what we deserve. Thank you for the forgiveness we find in Christ Jesus in whom we place our faith. Hear us as we pray in Jesus's name. Amen

89

For Your name's sake, O LORD, Pardon my iniquity, for it *is* great. (Psalm 25:11 NKJV)

Shepherd King of Righteousness, your name manifests your character. LORD God your character is love. LORD you give us unconditional love and save us from sins penalty. Although our sin is great, please pardon our guilt O LORD for your name's sake as we come before you with hearts broken because of our sinful actions. Thank you, LORD for your unending mercy. We pray this in the name of the Father, Son and Holy Spirit. Amen

90

that at the name of Jesus every knee should bow, in heaven and on earth and under the earth, (Philippians 2:10 NIV)

Lord Jesus, all people should worship and praise you for your redeeming sacrificial act on Calvary. Lord, there are many who think they must act under their own volition to gain a place for themselves in eternity. O how wrong they are. Lord at your name every knee shall bow either willingly or unwillingly. Lord, let the truth be revealed and all confess you as Lord so that none is lost. In the name of the Father, Son and Holy Spirit we pray. Amen

91

**For I am the LORD, your God, who takes hold of
your right hand and says to you, Do not fear; I will
help you. (Isaiah 41:13 NIV)**

O LORD Our God strengthen our faith as you hold our right hand and
guide us through the difficulties of this life. LORD, you are strong and
mighty; as we walk with you, alleviate our fears. This we pray in the
name of the Father, Son and Holy Spirit. Amen

92

**Oh, give thanks to the LORD, for *He is* good! For His
mercy *endures* forever. (Psalm 107:1 NKJV)**

LORD, for all you have already done. LORD, for all you are doing. And
LORD for what you will do, we give you thanks and praise, your love
endures forever. In Jesus's name we pray. Amen

93

**Yet I will rejoice in the LORD, I will joy in the God
of my salvation. (Habakkuk 3:18 NKJV)**

LORD God our savior, we are tested by many trials in life. There are
those LORD who ask the question, "LORD why do you allow this"?
Father God despite the trials and troubles we choose to rejoice in
you and be ever joyful while going through the tough times. Jesus
went through trials, so why should not we. Thank you, LORD for
being our comfort and sending Jesus our Savior. In Jesus's name we
pray. Amen

94

Let us therefore come boldly to the throne of grace, that we may obtain mercy and find grace to help in time of need. (Hebrews 4:16 NKJV)

Lord Jesus, you were tempted in the wilderness. We your disciples are being tempted daily by Satan as he seeks to seduce us with empty promises of power, wealth, desire fulfilled and other worldly enticements which seem attractive. Lord give your sympathetic help as we approach the throne of grace seeking your strength to stand in the face of such temptation. Lord in your mercy, hear our prayer. Amen

95

Praise be to the God and Father of our Lord Jesus Christ! In his great mercy he has given us new birth into a living hope through the resurrection of Jesus Christ from the dead, ⁴ and into an inheritance that can never perish, spoil or fade--kept in heaven for you, (1 Peter 1:3-4 NIV)

Almighty Father God, we have so much to be thankful for. Most of all we are thankful for the hope and great joy given us by the inheritance of the coming kingdom which was made possible through Christ Jesus. LORD, hear our prayer in Jesus's name. Amen

96

He saw that there was no one, he was appalled that there was no one to intervene; so his own arm worked salvation for him, and his own righteousness sustained him. (Isaiah 59:16 NIV)

LORD God Almighty, you looked throughout the earth and could find no one to intervene for mankind. There was no one righteous. Lord all you found was sin with its numerous offenses which testify against us. But LORD God of Love you worked out our salvation by your own arm. You sent Christ Jesus to be our intercessor, Savior and Redeemer. Through your righteousness Father God salvation has been made available to us. Thank you in Jesus's name. Amen

97

Nor is there salvation in any other, for there is no other name under heaven given among men by which we must be saved." (Acts 4:12 NKJV)

Lord Jesus, at your very name all must bow on earth, above the earth and below the earth. It is by your name that salvation comes to humans. Thank you, Lord, Our Savior, Our King, you are the Lamb of God who takes away the sins of the world. Amen

98

Finally, brethren, whatsoever things are true, whatsoever things *are* honest, whatsoever things *are* just, whatsoever things *are* pure, whatsoever things *are* lovely, whatsoever things *are* of good report; if *there be* any virtue, and if *there be* any praise, think on these things. (Philippians 4:8 KJV)

Father God in Heaven, you have given to your hand made servants your creation as a place of habitation. When we look around, we see your handiwork in all things; these all are praiseworthy. Help us O God to not focus on the creation but rather the Creator. Let our speech and actions be occupied by you O God our Father. Father God as we reflect on your goodness through Christ our Savior, help us to live wholesome, moral; spiritual lives as we strive to bring you glory. In Jesus's precious name we pray. Amen

99

But he said to me, "My grace is sufficient for you, for my power is made perfect in weakness." Therefore I will boast all the more gladly about my weaknesses, so that Christ's power may rest on me. (2 Corinthians 12:9 NIV)

LORD God Our Heavenly Father, We children of men think of ourselves as being strong in many aspects of life. LORD, help us to cast aside the illusionary façade of human strength as we make room for divine strength which allows knowledge and acceptance of your grace. We praise you LORD in Jesus's name. Amen

100

Since the children have flesh and blood, he too shared in their humanity so that by his death he might destroy him who holds the power of death-- that is, the devil. (Hebrews 2:14 NIV)

Thank you, Lord Jesus for sharing in our humanity. It was only through your death that death was destroyed, and Satan defeated. Lord we cannot escape the penalty of sin, but we need not fear death as we follow you with our whole heart, mind, body, and soul. Amen

101

His lord said to him, 'Well *done,* good and faithful servant; you were faithful over a few things, I will make you ruler over many things. Enter into the joy of your lord.' (Matthew 25:21 NKJV)

LORD God our Father, you have given us much in the way of knowledge, wealth, health, gifts of speaking, writing, and making beautiful music. LORD with the gifts you have an expectation that we should share them with one another. To whom much is given much is expected. O God help us to share our gifts for the benefit of the kingdom. This we pray in Jesus's name. Amen

102

They go from strength to strength, till each appears before God in Zion. (Psalm 84:7 NIV)

In the name of Jesus, we come before you the Great I AM. While we yet traverse through this life, we yearn to be in your presence LORD God Almighty. Help us to change from what we are into what you would have us to be. Only through divinely inspired spiritual growth can we be more Christ like, putting away self; depending on Christ Jesus for salvation. Lord, hear our prayer in Jesus's name. Amen

103

O LORD of hosts, Blessed *is* the man who trusts in You! (Psalm 84:12 NKJV)

O LORD Almighty, we see favor in the lives of some and lack in the lives of others. We choose to place our total trust in you because we know, blessed is the person who places their trust in you. This we pray in Jesus's name. Amen

104

I am the vine, you *are* the branches. He who abides in Me, and I in him, bears much fruit; for without Me you can do nothing. (John 15:5 NKJV)

Lord Jesus, you willingly allowed yourself to experience the pain inflicted on you by brutal men and then suffer death. All of this you permitted yourself to endure to bring us into fellowship with God our Father. Lord Jesus, bid the Father to prune the parts of our lives which need removing; that we might grow daily to be more like you as we walk towards eternity. Amen

105

A man's heart plans his way, But the LORD directs his steps. (Proverbs 16:9 NKJV)

Sovereign Lord our God, you work out everything according to your will. Merciful Father, make your will known to us and give us the power to carry it out–just as you did for Christ Jesus. In Jesus's name we pray. Amen

106

Love bears all things, believes all things, hopes all things, endures all things. (1Corinthians 13:7 ESV)

Lord Jesus our Redeemer, no greater love can one have than to lay down his life for another. You, Lord Jesus displayed such love for us on Calvary, thank you. Lord Jesus, help us to believe the best in all people, even when we see them at their worst. Help us to love as you love–because you are Love. In your name we pray. Amen

107

But as for you, speak the things which are proper for sound doctrine. (Titus 2:1 NKJV)

Lord Jesus, you are the Word and through you the word has been divinely inspired for the writers of the 66 books we call the Bible. Help us Lord to not turn away from sound doctrine as some are doing. Help us to not allow our feelings to come between your word and sound doctrine. Help us to receive and give careful instruction of the truth. This we pray in the name of the Father, Son and Holy Spirit. Amen

108

Therefore by Him let us continually offer the sacrifice of praise to God, that is, the fruit of *our* lips, giving thanks to His name. (Hebrews 13:15 NKJV)

Lord God the Holy One. In our brief lives you have completed so much on our behalf. Father God through Christ Jesus we praise you in the morning as we rise. We praise you during the day as we go about our business. We praise you in the night before we lay down to sleep. How wonderful you are and worthy to be praised. We praise you Father God in Jesus's name. Amen

109

While we look not at the things which are seen, but at the things which are not seen: for the things which are seen *are* temporal; but the things which are not seen *are* eternal. (2 Corinthians 4:18 KJV)

Lord God Heavenly Father, we live in a world which has many objects to capture our attention. Lord, help us to see with spiritual eyes, not the things visible but the things which are not seen. Help us to see that which is spiritually discerned. Looking at the visible cause's people to lose heart and not seek the eternal. Help us to look to the imperishable as we seek Christ Jesus with our whole body and soul. In Jesus's name we pray. Amen

110

Therefore, if anyone is in Christ, he is a new creation; the old has gone, the new has come! (2 Corinthians 5:17 NIV)

Lord Jesus, thank you for receiving us as heirs to the kingdom. Because of you we are new creations. Help us to walk as you have demonstrated to us so that the old perish and the new flourish. Amen

111

You will keep *him* in perfect peace, *Whose* mind *is* stayed *on You,* Because he trusts in You. (Isaiah 26:3 NKJV)

LORD God our Father. We come to you in the name of Jesus, thanking you for your promises towards us your chosen people. Thank you, Lord for peace amid the storms of life. We are determined to keep our mind stayed on you, seeking that perfect peace as we place our trust in you alone. In Jesus's name we pray. Amen

112

And over all these virtues put on love, which binds them all together in perfect unity. (Colossians 3:14 NIV)

Heavenly Father God, we come to you in the name of Jesus, asking that you divinely empower us to love each other so that we may live in perfect harmony as we await his return. This we pray in Jesus's name. Amen

113

Then he said, "Take the arrows," and the king took them. Elisha told him, "Strike the ground." He struck it three times and stopped. (2 Kings 13:18 NIV)

Our Father in Heaven, you allow your people to approach you in prayer with requests and offerings of thanksgiving for our desires as well as our needs of deliverance. LORD God we ask for many things and sometimes the manifestation of our request does not come as quickly as we would like. LORD your promise is that anything we ask in Jesus's name will be given. It is up to us Lord to ask continually, until you O Lord move on our behalf. Thank you, Lord that we can operate in faith and persistence to achieve the victory which you have promised. Help us to respond with enthusiasm as we seek your deliverance. This, we pray in Jesus's name. Amen

114

And you shall know the truth, and the truth shall make you free." (John 8:32 NKJV)

Lord Jesus, we jars of clay are captured and held hostage by the sin which so easily enslaves us. Because of our enslavement we were doomed to being lost to the second death; being cast into the lake of fire. Savior, you came into this world as the truth of God the Father's love. You came as the truth who gives eternal life to any who would place their faith in you. Lord Jesus, we thank you for affording us this opportunity to spend eternity with you in your prepared place for your prepared people. Amen

115

Let this mind be in you, which was also in Christ Jesus: (Philippians 2:5 KJV)

Gracious and Humble Lord, our minds are filled with the influences of the world. We often do not walk humbly as ego and pride seek precedence in many of our affairs. Lord Jesus, help us to have the same self-sacrificing attitude and love for others you demonstrated. Lord in your Mercy hear our Prayer. Amen

116

I will lift up mine eyes unto the hills, from whence cometh my help. (Psalm 121:1 KJV)

Lord God Almighty, we ask the rhetorical question, where does our help come from. Father God we know the answer. In the depths of our soul we know all good things come from you. We know that all peace, comfort, and strength comes' from you alone. Thank you for being faithful to us in all circumstances. This we pray in Jesus's name. Amen

117

The lips of the righteous know what is acceptable, but the mouth of the wicked what is perverse. (Proverbs 10:32 NRSV)

Lord God Almighty, we children of men speak words of comfort, blessing, encouragement, and curses. Help us Lord to eliminate the negative and accentuate the positive. This we pray in Jesus's name. Amen

118

Sing the glory of his name; make his praise glorious! (Psalm 66:2 NIV)

Lord, we people created by you lift our voices as we offer the fruit of our lips in praise. We praise you Lord, for cleansing us from our iniquity. Lord we praise you from the rising of the sun to the setting of the same. We praise you Lord for your precious blood which washes away our sin. Amen

119

Neither is there salvation in any other: for there is none other name under heaven given among men, whereby we must be saved. (Acts 4:12 KJV)

Gracious Lord Jesus, we people who are created by you seek to be saved and brought into paradise. Lord Jesus, there are many who say they must do good works in order to obtain salvation. Lord, there are those who claim salvation comes through proper praying, self-denial, merit accumulation and penance. Lord we pray for all who are searching after salvation in the wrong way. Your word says, "Salvation comes from Christ Jesus alone". Help those who are searching to find their way as they come to the knowledge of the truth. That truth being Jesus the Lamb of God who takes away the sins of the world. Amen

120

**Unto the upright there arises light in the darkness;
He is gracious, and full of compassion, and
righteous. (Psalm 112:4 NKJV)**

Heavenly Father our Lord and our God, there are many troubles which come our way in this life. Thank you, Lord, that as we place our faith in you–knowing who we are and whose we are those troubles cause us no fear. Thank you, Lord for being the God in whom we can completely place our trust. We know that you know us by name, and you are as near as us opening our mouths. Thank you, Lord. This we pray in Jesus's name. Amen

121

**Let us therefore come boldly to the throne of grace,
that we may obtain mercy and find grace to help in
time of need. (Hebrews 4:16 NKJV)**

Father God, we approach your throne of grace boldly in the matchless name of Jesus. LORD God we come seeking mercy for our brokenness. We desire a better way, yet sin is always crouching, dragging us into the underbrush of undesirable behavior. LORD, we are constantly in need of your forgiving grace. Thank you, LORD God, in Jesus's name for never turning your back on us as we walk yet on this side of eternity; thank you for grace. This we pray in Jesus's name. Amen

But now in Christ Jesus you who once were far off have been brought near by the blood of Christ. (Ephesians 2:13 NKJV)

LORD, we were once at odds with you because of sin. Now through Christ Jesus we have been brought near to you, God our Father. Thank you, Lord Jesus for shedding your blood to redeem us. LORD Hear our Prayer in the name of the Father, Son and Holy Spirit. Amen

We have not received the spirit of the world but the Spirit who is from God, that we may understand what God has freely given us. (1 Corinthians 2:12 NIV)

LORD God our Heavenly Creator, you have imparted the spirit of life into each of your hand made servants. LORD we have your spirit dwelling within each of us, not the spirit of this world. LORD let your spirit within increase, giving us Christ like behavior as we interact with all people. Father God–forgive us when we attempt to supersede the spirit through worldly actions. LORD in your mercy, hear our prayer as we pray this in Jesus's name. Amen

So then neither he who plants is anything, nor he who waters, but God who gives the increase. (1 Corinthians 3:7 NKJV)

Lord God our Father in Heaven, as we seek to join you in your work of saving lost souls help us to understand that the part, we play has its place in the process of salvation. Lord, our part is directing people to Christ, we cannot save anyone; the act of saving is Christ's alone. Let us O God through our testimony help others to know Christ, as your

Spirit draws them to him. Father God–bless our efforts as we work for the kingdom. In Jesus's name we pray. Amen

125

Then Samuel took a stone and set it up between Mizpah and Shen. He named it Ebenezer, saying, "Thus far has the LORD helped us." (1 Samuel 7:12 NIV)

Lord, you are the stone which has fallen upon and broken the back of sin in our lives. How can we ever offer enough thanks and praise for your mighty works? In the name of the Father, Son and Holy Spirit we pray. Amen

126

So, whether you eat or drink, or whatever you do, do everything for the glory of God. (1 Corinthians 10:31 NRSV)

LORD God of Glory, there are times in this life we live, when it is a struggle to make it through the day. LORD this life is a gift from you to be cherished not endured. Grant us comfort through knowing you as our comforter. LORD help us to glorify you in all we say, think and do. LORD let our hearts find rest in you through Christ Jesus. In Jesus's name we pray. Amen

127

Before they call I will answer, while they are yet speaking I will hear. (Isaiah 65:24 NRSV)

Father God, as we approach each new day, we ask that you hear our prayers. LORD God hear our hearts before we come to you in prayer. LORD act on our requests for healing both spiritually and physically.

LORD, restore our broken relationships. LORD, give us forgiving hearts. Hear our hearts and cleanse them of the impurities of the world. Father God let us be changed to resemble Christ as we advance in this life. This we ask in Jesus's name. Amen

128

The heavens declare the glory of God; the skies proclaim the work of his hands. (Psalm 19:1 NIV)

LORD, we thank you for showing yourself daily and constantly. LORD, we see you in the morning sunrise. LORD we hear you in the kind words of strangers and friends. LORD we feel you in the touch of loved ones and the kiss of a child. LORD you touch our hearts with the songs of birds as well as those on the airwaves. LORD, you comfort us as we fall asleep for the night. We thank you LORD through Jesus for always reminding us of your constant presence. Amen

129

May the favor of the Lord our God rest upon us; establish the work of our hands for us-- yes, establish the work of our hands. (Psalm 90:17 NIV)

Father God in Heaven grant us your favor that we may be productive as we work in the kingdom directing those who are still lost to Christ Jesus, the savior of all mankind. Lord please bless our work. In Jesus's name we pray. Amen

130

Not to us, O LORD, not to us but to your name be the glory, because of your love and faithfulness. (Psalm 115:1 NIV)

Gracious LORD our God, you bear with your people who at times seek precedence over you by taking the focus from you and placing it on themselves. Father, as you see this in us, wash us clean of selfishness and help us to be Christ centered that we may give glory to you alone. Lord, thank you for the blood which cleanses us of our sin. Father God, this we pray in Jesus's name. Amen

131

His divine power has given us everything we need for life and godliness through our knowledge of him who called us by his own glory and goodness. (2 Peter 1:3 NIV)

O Lord our God, it is through your divine power that we have life and can even accept godliness. Without you O Lord we would be forever lost. Thank you for always being present in our lives giving us knowledge of you as you direct us to excellence and eventually to eternal glory with you. Amen

132

I do not understand what I do. For what I want to do I do not do, but what I hate I do. (Romans 7:15 NIV)

Lord God our Father, you know everything we have said, thought and done. Lord you know what we should have done, meant to do, forgot to do, refused to do and was afraid to do. Lord we fail in so many ways when we in our doing fail to glorify you. Help us to do the good you would have us do, not the bad our flesh desires to do. Forgive us for Jesus's sake. Amen

133

This is the day the LORD has made; let us rejoice and be glad in it. (Psalm 118:24 NIV)

Thank you, Father God for this new day which you have made. LORD this is a day we never saw before and shall never see again. Help us to be glad and rejoice in it and to glorify you as we move through it. This we pray in Jesus's name. Amen

134

Refrain from anger and turn from wrath; do not fret--it leads only to evil. (Psalm 37:8 NIV)

Lord God of Comfort and Peace, anger and rage are often the companions of us children of men. Lord Jesus as you hung on the cross of Calvary you did not display anger even towards those who mocked and spit on you. Lord, you asked that they be forgiven due to their lack of understanding. Lord, we ask that this same spirit of tolerance be given us. Lord we ask that anger in our hearts be removed that your Word may indwell our hearts as we intermingle with other human beings. Lord in your mercy, hear our prayer. Amen

135

A good name is more desirable than great riches; to be esteemed is better than silver or gold. (Proverbs 22:1 NIV)

Precious Lord, the name of Jesus is a name which holds the keys of salvation for all of mankind. Lord, we children of men wish to have a good name which draws people to Christ Jesus by seeing our actions. Help us to live a godly life with our name corresponding to Christ like living. This we pray in the name of the Father, Son and Holy Spirit. Amen

136

Humble yourselves in the sight of the Lord, and he shall lift you up. (James 4:10 KJV)

Lord God our Father, thank you for the good you have given us in life, all good things come from you. Lord do not let those things cause us to lose focus of you. Lord do not let us become so self-absorbed that when we are wrong, we are not willing to change. Lord, help us to be easy to live with as we direct our attention to you and not inward towards self. Lord in your mercy, help us to be humble. This we pray in Jesus's name. Amen

137

If anyone thinks he is something when he is nothing, he deceives himself. (Galatians 6:3 NIV)

Lord God who is Wisdom, do not allow pride to overtake us your people. Holy Spirit teach us humility that we do not deceive ourselves with false grandiosity. This we pray in the name of Jesus. Amen

138

For the LORD your God is God of gods and Lord of lords, the great God, mighty and awesome, who shows no partiality and accepts no bribes. (Deuteronomy 10:17 NIV)

God of gods, you are Mighty and Awesome; this is attributed to you alone. We love you Lord, with an unyielding love which causes our hearts to glow–at the thought of the reciprocated love you return to all your people. LORD, we thank you that no human being regardless of race creed or color is rejected by you. We thank you that your favor cannot be purchased by any but is your free, gift to mankind. Lord, help us to love our fellow human beings in like manner. This we pray in the name of the Father, Son and Holy Spirit. Amen

139

He cuts off every branch in me that bears no fruit, while every branch that does bear fruit he prunes so that it will be even more fruitful. (John 15:2 NIV)

Lord of the Harvest, we are the branches, you are the vine. We need pruning that we may become fruitful; producing a yield of Christ likeness which draws people into the kingdom as they seek to know Christ in his fullness and truth. Remove from us all that is unproductive, allow the re-growth of Christ likeness to be virtuous. This we pray in the name of the Father, Son and Holy Spirit. Amen

140

Do you not say, 'Four months more and then the harvest'? I tell you, open your eyes and look at the fields! They are ripe for harvest. (John 4:35 NIV)

Lord God of the Harvest, we your created people are all known by you. Lord some of us know you as Savior and others do not. The others who do not know you as savior just know you as God. Lord help us to be willing workers in the kingdom, who go out and harvest as we direct those in the harvest field to Christ. This we pray in Jesus's name. Amen

141

It is because of him that you are in Christ Jesus, who has become for us wisdom from God--that is, our righteousness, holiness and redemption. (1 Corinthians 1:30 NIV)

O God, we speak to you in complete confidence because all good things come from you. Thank you that the Holy Spirit has revealed the truth for many who would receive it, that righteousness, salvation, and redemption come through Christ Jesus alone. Many are yet unwise as they attempt to gain for themselves salvation by the works of their hands. Thank you for the wisdom given through the Holy Spirit to show the true way to eternal life, which is Christ Jesus. This we pray in the name of the Father, Son and Holy Spirit. Amen

142

How can a young man keep his way pure? By living according to your word. (Psalm 119:9 NIV)

Lord God our Father, we have all walked in the way of lustful flesh. There were times when we wanted what we wanted regardless of who was hurt in the process. LORD we thank you for deliverance from self as we are led by your Spirit to reject gratifying the cravings of the sinful nature. Lord in your Mercy hear our prayer. Amen

143

Through him you believe in God, who raised him from the dead and glorified him, and so your faith and hope are in God. (1 Peter 1:21 NIV)

God of Redemption, it is through the sacrificial act of Christ Jesus that we now know and believe–that you are a loving and caring God who provides for our wellbeing. Father God, as you raised Christ from the dead glorifying him, you illustrated that you are awesome and mighty, loving us beyond measure. Thank you in Jesus's name. Amen

144

The righteous man leads a blameless life; blessed are his children after him. (Proverbs 20:7 NIV)

Our Father who is in Heaven, we children of men seek to be righteous as we dwell on this earth attempting to follow the path Christ has laid out before us. The sad truth Lord is that we fail; we sin in thought, word and deed. Help us Lord to live a life which expresses a legacy of excellence, encouragement, and love. Thank you, Lord Jesus that our righteousness comes through you. Lord, bless our offspring after us. This we ask in Jesus's name. Amen

145

Whoever does not love does not know God, because God is love. (1 John 4:8 NIV)

Lord God, you are the ultimate expression of love. Father God show us how to love as you love us, without added conditions, but freely as we open our hearts to one another. This we pray through Christ Jesus who came into the world that through him we would live out love's redemptive plan. Amen

146

And the second is like it: 'Love your neighbor as yourself.' (Matthew 22:39 NIV)

Lord God you are love. Father, we cannot live on this earth in singularity. Lord, we need one another. You made us as social beings, people who survive through interaction with one another as parts of the living body of Christ. Lord God help us to be loving brothers and sisters. This we pray in Jesus's name. Amen

147

And walk in love, as Christ also has loved us and given Himself for us, an offering and a sacrifice to God for a sweet-smelling aroma. (Ephesians 5:2 NKJV)

Lord Jesus, how can we thank you for your ultimate gift of love as you gave yourself up for us—as a fragrant offering and sacrifice to God our

Father. Because of your love we seek to live a life of love towards one another, help us to do so. We pray this, in the name of the Father, Son and Holy Spirit. Amen

148

And hope does not disappoint us, because God has poured out his love into our hearts by the Holy Spirit, whom he has given us. (Romans 5:5 NIV)

Lord God of Hope, you have poured into our hearts the hope of salvation–by the love which is in our hearts nurtured through the Holy Spirit. Thank you in Jesus's name that the Holy Spirit was sent to us. Amen

149

I want to know Christ and the power of his resurrection and the fellowship of sharing in his sufferings, becoming like him in his death, and so, somehow, to attain to the resurrection from the dead. (Philippians 3:10-11 NIV)

Lord Jesus, we want to know you intimately and the power of your resurrection. Lord Jesus we know that as we place our faith in you alone, we have a right relationship with our Father God. Thank you, Lord that through you we will receive a resurrection into eternal life. We pray through the Father, Son and Holy Spirit. Amen

150

Find rest, O my soul, in God alone; my hope comes from him. (Psalm 62:5 NIV)

Lord God Heavenly Father, we approach you in the name of Jesus. In you alone LORD can we find rest for our weary minds. LORD, the world bombards us with many trials and tribulations. Father God, if we place our focus on you and not our surroundings, we can walk in the blessed hope which comes through you alone. Help us never forget this. This we pray in Jesus's name. Amen

151

As it is written: *"There is none righteous, no, not one;* (Romans 3:10 NKJV)

Father God, I know I am sinful. I sin by what I do, and I sin by what I leave undone. Father God I know I needed Christ Jesus and the suffering and death he endured on my behalf. LORD through Christ's work on the cross I am redeemed and now have eternal life awaiting me. Thank you, in the name of the Father, Son and Holy Ghost. Amen

152

who comforts us in all our tribulation, that we may be able to comfort those who are in any trouble, with the comfort with which we ourselves are comforted by God. (2 Corinthians 1:4 NKJV)

Lord God of comfort, as you–through Christ Jesus have comforted us in our times of suffering, help us to comfort others with that same comfort that they may come to know Christ Jesus through our actions. This we pray in Jesus's name. Amen

153

And we, who with unveiled faces all reflect the Lord's glory, are being transformed into his likeness with ever-increasing glory, which comes from the Lord, who is the Spirit. (2 Corinthians 3:18 NIV)

Lord Jesus, we are gradually being transformed into your likeness. Lord the process is slow because of our flirting with sin. Lord, through the power of the Holy Spirit help us reject sin as we are being sanctified daily. Lord Jesus, please change us daily into your image that we may become more like you each day. Lord in your Mercy hear our prayer. Amen

154

Set your minds on things above, not on earthly things. (Colossians 3:2 NIV)

Lord God our Creator, we live on this world the planet earth. We have established a perception of value based upon worldly assets which we seek to acquire. Lord, instill in your people the importance of things not of this world but from above. This world and all it encompass will one day be consumed and melt away. Help us to set our minds on things above, not earthly things. This we pray in Jesus's name. Amen

155

**The steps of a *good* man are ordered by the LORD,
And He delights in his way. (Psalm 37:23 NKJV)**

Lord God Almighty, you are awesome and powerful. LORD, you watch over all your creation with great care. LORD, you know our coming and going. LORD, order our steps as we proceed throughout each day that our steps not lead us astray. Help us LORD to walk in the paths of righteousness that we may bring glory to you in our doing so. This we pray in Jesus's name. Amen

156

to slander no one, to be peaceable and considerate, and to show true humility toward all men. (Titus 3:2 NIV)

Heavenly Father God, we children of men, cast subjective opinions regarding one another. Help us to not speak ill of one another but to embrace one another in Christian love. This we pray in Jesus's name. Amen

157

Rather, we have renounced secret and shameful ways; we do not use deception, nor do we distort the word of God. On the contrary, by setting forth the truth plainly we commend ourselves to every man's conscience in the sight of God. (2 Corinthians 4:2 NIV)

LORD God of truth, we your hand made servants who profess Christianity are making every effort to reject misrepresenting you, and our Lord and Savior Jesus Christ. LORD, the shameful ways of those who distort the reality of your word we refute since it is not truth. Reinforce us as we continue our Christian walk, sharing the pure truth of your word as you have revealed it to us. Lord in your mercy, hear our prayer. Amen

158

And Abraham called the name of that place Jehovahjireh: as it is said *to* this day, In the mount of the LORD it shall be seen. (Genesis 22:14 KJV)

LORD God Heavenly Father, we acknowledge your attribute of Jehovah Jireh, you are our provider. Without you Lord we have nothing. Through you Lord we have everything needed. Thank you, Lord. In Jesus's name we pray this. Amen

159

Therefore we do not lose heart. Though outwardly we are wasting away, yet inwardly we are being renewed day by day. (2 Corinthians 4:16 NIV)

Lord God Heavenly Father, although our outward bodies age and decline in ability, our inward person grows more in Christian strength each day. Thank you, Father God that our inward person receives fresh and renewed strength each day. Thank you, LORD for the unseen which manifests itself as the wisdom of years you have given us. LORD we pray this in the name of the Father, Son and Holy Spirit. Amen

160

Dear friends, I urge you, as aliens and strangers in the world, to abstain from sinful desires, which war against your soul. (1 Peter 2:11 NIV)

Lord Jesus, we children of men are saddled with all sorts of carnal passions. Lord, send the Holy Spirit we pray to help us subdue unrighteous passion which has the possibility of leading us to even greater sinful activity. Lord, we can do this through you who strengthens' us and the Holy Spirit who teaches us. Lord in your mercy, hear our prayer. Amen

161

and if you call out for insight and cry aloud for understanding, and if you look for it as for silver and search for it as for hidden treasure, then you will understand the fear of the LORD and find the knowledge of God. (Proverbs 2:3-5 NIV)

Father God, through your Holy Spirit empower us to seek knowledge of your word and the wisdom it imparts with the same determination of a prospector mining silver or gold. This we pray in Jesus's name. Amen

162

Those who trust in the LORD are like Mount Zion, which cannot be shaken but endures forever. (Psalm 125:1 NIV)

Lord, we want to place our total trust in you so that we may not be shaken in times of trouble but instead stand steadfast and unmovable as the mountains. Lord, help us to accomplish this. Lord, forgive our Swiss cheese faith, which is not solid but full of holes. This we pray in the name of the Father, Son and Holy Spirit. Amen

163

Only be careful, and watch yourselves closely so that you do not forget the things your eyes have seen or let them slip from your heart as long as you live. Teach them to your children and to their children after them. (Deuteronomy 4:9 NIV)

Lord God Almighty, we children of men watch each other and watch the affairs in our lives closely. Father God, where we fall short is in watching self. Father God help us through your Spirit to be more diligent in watching ourselves and living more in alignment with your precious word which directs us to life. Lord, help us to teach these truths to our children and our children's, children. This we pray in Jesus's Holy name. Amen

164

O LORD, you have searched me and you know me. (Psalm 139:1 NIV)

O Lord our God, you have known us before we were born. Lord, you knew how our lives would turn out before we even breathed our first breath. Lord, help us to glorify you through Christ Jesus in all our thoughts, words, and deeds. Correct us, we pray if our heart and mind attempt to lead us in the wrong path. This we pray in Jesus's name. Amen

And the four beasts had each of them six wings about *him*; and *they were* full of eyes within: and they rest not day and night, saying, Holy, holy, holy, Lord God Almighty, which was, and is, and is to come. (Revelation 4:8 KJV)

O Lord God, you are Holy. Transform us here on earth to follow in the train of your holiness, thereby making this world a better place for all. In your Trinity, Holy, Holy, Holy you are. This we pray in the name of the Father, Son and Holy Spirit. Amen

***It is* good for me that I have been afflicted, That I may learn Your statutes. (Psalm 119:71 NKJV)**

Lord God Heavenly Father, life has presented many of us with difficulties which we thought we would not survive. For some Lord it was substance abuse, sexual abuse, lascivious behavior, dishonesty, prejudice, arrogance, and a multitude of other sinful human afflictions. Father God as we are no longer held in bondage to those past afflictions, we can see your promise of "never again" as you told Noah concerning the flood waters. Thank you for bringing us through the heartaches of the past. We can look back and say it was good that we were afflicted. Now as we stand in the shadow of the cross, Father God we are living examples of your promise which says, "you are mine, fear not". We thank you in the name of Jesus. Amen

So shall My word be that goes forth from My mouth; It shall not return to Me void, But it shall accomplish what I please, And it shall prosper *in the thing* for which I sent it. (Isaiah 55:11 NKJV)

Father God, there are times when we read and study your word but only days later, we cannot quote verbatim that scripture. Father God, your word as you have said shall not return to you void without accomplishing its purpose. Lord, let your word work abundantly in us. Help us to retain and give us the ability to repeat what we have read so we can share that word with a sin sick and dying world. This we pray in the name of the Father, Son and Holy Spirit. Amen

168

The truly righteous man attains life, but he who pursues evil goes to his death. (Proverbs 11:19 NIV)

Gracious Father God, we each have the opportunity for eternal life through Christ Jesus, who died that through him we could be redeemed for eternity. Help us Lord to follow your statutes and not those of the world. Lord we seek life in Christ not death, help us to grasp the opportunity in Christ. Lord let all find their righteousness in Christ, that none be lost. This is our prayer and we pray it in Jesus's name. Amen

169

My little children, let us not love in word, neither in tongue; but in deed and in truth. (1 John 3:18 KJV)

Lord Jesus, let us not walk around with empty words of love which have no substance. Lord Grant us the power to demonstrate an unyielding love as you did through your deeds. Lord, in your mercy hear our prayer. Amen

170

For those God foreknew he also predestined to be conformed to the likeness of his Son, that he might be the firstborn among many brothers. (Romans 8:29 NIV)

Lord God Heavenly Father, you began working out your plan of salvation for us before we were formed in our mother's womb. Because you were working out your plan for salvation, we can look upon the cross as the anchor in that plan. Lord, we seek daily to be conformed to the image of Christ. Help us through the Holy Spirit to achieve this. In Christ Jesus we pray. Amen

171

But my God shall supply all your need according to his riches in glory by Christ Jesus. (Philippians 4:19 KJV)

Lord God our Father, you will meet all our daily needs according to your word. Thank you for your most glorious riches in Christ Jesus, in whose name we pray. Amen

172

When I saw him, I fell at his feet as though dead. Then he placed his right hand on me and said: "Do not be afraid. I am the First and the Last. (Revelation 1:17 NIV)

Lord Jesus our Savior, you are our beginning and you are our ending. Lord, you touch us with your Gospel which comforts us and removes fear as we live in this convoluted world. Lord Jesus we await the day when you will carry us home to that lasting place of eternal joy which we will share with you. Lord in your mercy, hear our prayer. Amen

173

God made him who had no sin to be sin for us, so that in him we might become the righteousness of God. (2 Corinthians 5:21 NIV)

Lord Jesus our Redeemer, thank you for taking on the sins of the world which now offers us eternal life. Forgive us for falling short even though we are aware of the events which took place leading to the cross on Calvary. Strengthen us to battle our sinful nature. Lord, hear our prayer. Amen

174

Better is one day in your courts than a thousand elsewhere; I would rather be a doorkeeper in the house of my God than dwell in the tents of the wicked. (Psalm 84:10 NIV)

Lord God our Heavenly Father, spending a day with you is far better than a thousand elsewhere. Lord, you are our rock and fortress, our comfort, and our strength. Lord, to spend a day in your sanctuary quenches our thirst and feeds our hunger; it soothes our sin sick souls. Lord God, we would rather be doorkeepers in your house than to dwell with the unrighteous of this world. Lord in your mercy, hear our prayer. Amen

175

Get rid of all bitterness, rage and anger, brawling and slander, along with every form of malice. (Ephesians 4:31 NIV)

Gracious, forgiving, and compassionate Father God, we children of men become inflamed by the slightest infraction of what we subjectively believe to be proper. Father God, what we deem proper pales in comparison to your interpretation of proper. Father God remove the rage, anger, malice, and slander from us. Replace those things with your Holy Spirit of peace which teaches proper interaction with all other people. This we pray in Jesus's name. Amen

176

O LORD Almighty, blessed is the man who trusts in you. (Psalm 84:12 NIV)

Lord God Heavenly Father, those who place their trust in you are indeed the blessed of the earth. Thank you, Lord, for allowing our existence to be summed up in just six words, "I am blessed of the Lord". Amen

177

And by that will, we have been made holy through the sacrifice of the body of Jesus Christ once for all. (Hebrews 10:10 NIV)

Lord—no more does mankind need to offer up animals as a blood sacrifice for the atonement of sins. You Lord have made the ultimate sacrifice in your blood to redeem us as your own. Thank you, Lord Jesus for being the Lamb of God who takes away the sins of the world. This we pray in the name of the Father, Son and Holy Spirit. Amen

178

Trust in him at all times, O people; pour out your hearts to him, for God is our refuge. Selah (Psalm 62:8 NIV)

Gracious God our Father, who else can we go to as we pour out from the depths of our hearts revealing who and what we really are. You alone O God is the one in whom we can trust in making ourselves vulnerable by exposing our true nature. Thank you, Lord God for being our refuge and burden bearer. We offer our prayer in Jesus's name. Amen

179

Let the righteous rejoice in the LORD and take refuge in him; let all the upright in heart praise him! (Psalm 64:10 NIV)

Merciful Lord, we rejoice in your unfailing love as we attempt to walk in righteousness. Lord Jesus, our righteousness is found in you. Lord Jesus, we place our trust in you as you cleanse our hearts of unrighteousness; we lift your name in praise. Amen

180

If we live, we live to the Lord; and if we die, we die to the Lord. So, whether we live or die, we belong to the Lord. (Romans 14:8 NIV)

Living and Eternal Lord God who created all things, we belong to you despite our shortcomings, defects, and faults. You love us with an everlasting love. Thank you, Lord for loving us as we live here on this earth and thank you for receiving us when we die and leave this earth. We belong to you, you who have created us for yourself. We praise you Lord. Amen

181

Then we will not turn away from you; revive us, and we will call on your name. (Psalm 80:18 NIV)

O LORD our God, we vow to trust in you alone. In you LORD we seek the refreshing of spirit which you alone can give. Renew us LORD, as you remove our sinful nature and fill us with the revitalization of your Holy Spirit. This we pray in Jesus's name. Amen

182

**he does not treat us as our sins deserve or repay
us according to our iniquities. (Psalm 103:10 NIV)**

God of Grace and Mercy, you do not treat us according to what our sins deserve. Please Lord, forgive us our failings. Lord, help us to treat one another in like manner, that your love may be displayed through us. In this the world may know we are Christians by our love for all mankind. This we pray in Jesus's name. Amen

183

**What then? Shall we sin because we are not under law
but under grace? By no means! (Romans 6:15 NIV)**

Lord of Grace and Compassion, despite our acting out in a worldly manner you demonstrate your grace in our lives daily. How can we not try to show kindness to one another as we seek to emulate the benevolence of your love in our lives? Lord, hear our prayer and the contrition emanating from within our hearts. We pray this in the name of the Father, Son and Holy Spirit. Amen

184

**Then Peter began to speak: "I now realize how true it
is that God does not show favoritism. (Acts 10:34 NIV)**

Father God, you look upon your created people and see us individually, yet you give us each the same opportunity. LORD you show no bias, favoritism, or no penchant towards one who seeks spiritual mindedness or lack towards one who has yet to come to the knowledge of the truth. Because of your steadfast love we each have the same prospect for eternal life through Christ Jesus. Thank you, LORD in Jesus's name. Amen

185

Therefore, since we are surrounded by such a great cloud of witnesses, let us throw off everything that hinders and the sin that so easily entangles, and let us run with perseverance the race marked out for us. (Hebrews 12:1 NIV)

O Lord our God, we carry many burdens as we pass through this life. Most all are self-imposed by what we allow into our lives. Lord, help us lay aside the burdens which hinder us from running the race that is set before us. Lord in your mercy, hear our prayer. Amen

186

Do not cast me from your presence or take your Holy Spirit from me. (Psalm 51:11 NIV)

Lord God of Mercy, without you we are lost souls without direction, please never send us away from your presence. Lord, never remove your Holy Spirit but allow him to teach us and use us to reach out to others who do not yet know you. Lord we stand in agreement praying this prayer. And we pray this in Jesus's name. Amen

187

Yet a time is coming and has now come when the true worshipers will worship the Father in spirit and truth, for they are the kind of worshipers the Father seeks. (John 4:23 NIV)

Father God in Heaven, we children of men often say we worship you with our whole hearts. Upon closer examination it is found we limit our reverence for you through our neglect of forgiving, loving, and caring for each other as your decree demands. Help us O God to worship you right now in Spirit and Truth since these are the type worshippers you desire. This we pray in Jesus's name. Amen

188

And God will wipe away every tear from their eyes; there shall be no more death, nor sorrow, nor crying. There shall be no more pain, for the former things have passed away." (Revelation 21:4 NKJV)

Lord Jesus, we live in a world of trouble, sorrow, pain, sighing, crying and dying which, we bring upon ourselves. We know that because of you, Christ Jesus–we will one day be brought to the place where there will be no more of these things and every tear will be wiped away from our eyes. Lord, until that day–if it be your Holy Will, grant us peace. This we stand in agreement and pray for in the name of the Father, Son and Holy Spirit. Amen

189

My help *comes* from the LORD, Who made heaven and earth. (Psalm 121:2 NKJV)

Lord, we children of men often take upon ourselves the mantle of "I can do this on my own". Lord, we always fail when we do not first seek you and the help which comes from you. Lord, please forgive our arrogance as we seek self-sufficiency. Help us to always look to you our omnipotent God. Lord in your Mercy–hear our prayer. Amen

190

for it is God who works in you both to will and to do for *His* good pleasure. (Philippians 2:13 NKJV)

Lord God our Head, you have planned our lives and bless that initiative according to your will not ours. Lord you have given us talents and placed into our hearts what is necessary to accomplish your good and perfect will. Use us daily Lord in the building of your kingdom. Help us to glorify you through our efforts. This we pray in Jesus's Holy name. Amen

191

Oh, give thanks to the LORD, for *He is* good! For His mercy *endures* forever. (1 Chronicles 16:34 NKJV)

Thank you, Lord for another day. Thank you for another opportunity to do better. Thank you for not giving us what we deserve. Thank you for your unfailing love. Thank you for dying as our mediator Jesus, that we might be found righteous in the sight of God the Father. Thank you, Lord Jesus, we praise your precious name. Amen

192

But one is tempted by one's own desire, being lured and enticed by it. (James 1:14 NRSV)

Father God, there are many things this world offers which can come between us and you. LORD, it is by our personal lust's that we remove ourselves from appropriate relationship with you. LORD, the temptations are numerous, seductive, and appealing. LORD, help us to resist and not be drawn away from you by the empty promises of that which is not your perfect gift, which leads to sin. This is our prayer in Jesus's name. Amen

193

Peace I leave with you; my peace I give to you. I do not give to you as the world gives. Do not let your hearts be troubled, and do not let them be afraid. (John 14:27 NRSV)

Gracious Lord, you came that we might have peace with our conscience towards God the Father. Lord Jesus, thank you for the peace you give, not as the world gives conditional peace but as our divine savior who gives unconditional eternal peace. Because of your peace we have rest at night and peace during our daily activities. Thank you, Lord for peace as only you can give. Amen

194

Brothers, think of what you were when you were called. Not many of you were wise by human standards; not many were influential; not many were of noble birth. (1 Corinthians 1:26 NIV)

Christ Jesus our Compassionate Shepherd. We often stray from the path of righteousness, yet with gentle love and compassion you return us to the fold. Lord, although we sometimes look like and act like weeds choking out harmony among the populace, you see roses which give off an inviting fragrance. Lord, where we are sinful in thought, word and deed–you see a restored people. Lord, you bring great joy to the people of this world by not seeing us as we are but as you intend us to be. Thank you. Amen

195

How great is your goodness, which you have stored up for those who fear you, which you bestow in the sight of men on those who take refuge in you. (Psalm 31:19 NIV)

Lord God of Goodness, you bless those who take refuge in you and stand in awe of you in the presence of all to see. All we can say is "How great is your Goodness". This we pray with grateful hearts in the name of Jesus. Amen

196

Now these things became our examples, to the intent that we should not lust after evil things as they also lusted. (1 Corinthians 10:6 NKJV)

Lord God Heavenly Father, there are many things which we your handmade servants seek after. Father God in our seeking please do not allow us to fall into idolatry and other inappropriate behavior. Father God help us to place no one and nothing above our worship of you. This we pray in Jesus's name. Amen

197

He answered and said, "Whether He is a sinner *or not* I do not know. One thing I know: that though I was blind, now I see." (John 9:25 NKJV)

Lord, it is amazing that although we once walked in darkness you pierced that darkness with your revealing light–which gives direction towards life. Lord, there was a time we did not know you but now we do. "We once were blind but now we see". O Lord–hear our prayer in the name of the Father, Son and Holy Spirit. Amen

198

for anyone who enters God's rest also rests from his own work, just as God did from his. (Hebrews 4:10 NIV)

Lord of the Sabbath, who gives his people rest. Help us O Lord to take advantage of your example of taking time to rest. Lord, let us not be so caught up in the activities of life that rest eludes us. This is our prayer, in Jesus's name. Amen

199

For the word of God *is* living and powerful, and sharper than any two-edged sword, piercing even to the division of soul and spirit, and of joints and marrow, and is a discerner of the thoughts and intents of the heart. (Hebrews 4:12 NKJV)

Heavenly Father God, your word gives us guidance as we study, meditate, and attempt to live out your word in our everyday lives. Father God, your word judges the thoughts and attitudes of the heart. Lord God cleanse our hearts that our hearts be found acceptable in your sight. This we pray in Jesus's name. Amen

200

But if we walk in the light as He is in the light, we have fellowship with one another, and the blood of Jesus Christ His Son cleanses us from all sin. (1 John 1:7 NKJV)

Lord Jesus, we seek to walk in the light. Lord, you are the light of the World. We ask that you shine all around us, bringing us into fellowship with fellow believers. Your blood has cleansed us from all sin, and through you the path to eternal life has been illuminated. Lord in your mercy, hear our prayer. Amen

201

For it will come upon all those who live on the face of the whole earth. (Luke 21:35 NIV)

O Lord, we know that the day is approaching when you will return to receive to yourself all of those who have placed their faith in you and belong to you. Lord, we also know that those who do not know you will be lost. Lord, help those of us who know you to go and witness to those who have yet to know you, so that they too may be saved. Lord in your Mercy hear our prayer. Amen

202

But you will receive power when the Holy Spirit comes on you; and you will be my witnesses in Jerusalem, and in all Judea and Samaria, and to the ends of the earth." (Acts 1:8 NIV)

Holy Lord empower us with your Holy Spirit to be your Redeemed witnesses who testify of your goodness. Help us who share your Gospel message with those who do not understand your unfailing love. Lord remove the spirit of fear which hinders us from being those witnesses, who tell of your act of Love which occurred by you taking on the death we deserve. Lord Jesus, remove the fear, give us the power, and help us to proclaim with determination our individual testimonies of you coming into our lives. Amen

203

The apostles said to the Lord, "Increase our faith!" (Luke 17:5 NIV)

O Lord, we ask that you increase our faith. Lord, we do not want faith which calls on the yesterdays of life saying, "if only I could have, or I should have". Lord, we do not want faith that seeks some unseen future which says, "tomorrow is going to be better than today". Lord, please give us a right now faith which operates in the here and now saying "I know that through the Power of my God everything is alright, right now regardless of how things look". Lord, we are seeking a faith which is active and sure. This is our prayer in Jesus's name. Amen

204

Turn my eyes away from worthless things; preserve my life according to your word. (Psalm 119:37 NIV)

Eternal King, we approach you in the name of Jesus our Lord and Savior. LORD God there are so many distractions in this world which can quickly cause us to miss what is enormously important. Father, this world has many trinkets which we see causing us to lose our focus of you. LORD God let your Spirit fall fresh upon us as we desire to remain focused on you through Christ Jesus who makes all things possible. Give us focus we pray in the name of the Father, Son and Holy Spirit. Amen

205

his work will be shown for what it is, because the Day will bring it to light. It will be revealed with fire, and the fire will test the quality of each man's work. (1 Corinthians 3:13 NIV)

Lord God Almighty, the day is coming when all people shall stand in judgment before you. O God we want to live pure and undefiled lives, yet we stumble and fall, forgive us. Thank you for the grace afforded us through Christ Jesus which was won at Calvary. Thank you that we can now stand as those redeemed by the blood of the Lamb. This we pray with grateful hearts in Jesus's name. Amen

206

Oh, that their hearts would be inclined to fear me and keep all my commands always, so that it might go well with them and their children forever! (Deuteronomy 5:29 NIV)

LORD God our Father, you alone are awesome and mighty, merciful and loving. O LORD how much better life would be if we were always obedient to your will for our lives. LORD we would live in peace and harmony as we receive the many blessings which we now miss because of disobedience. LORD everything you ask us to do is that life might go well with us. Help us O LORD to live with hearts turned to your will and your ways. This we pray in Jesus's name. Amen

207

But the very hairs of your head are all numbered. (Matthew 10:30 NKJV)

O God, we are fully yours. You created us in our mother's womb. You knitted together the sinew which gives us composition. O God, we are so very well known by you that you have numbered the very hairs of our heads. It is amazing Father God that you know us and love us so intimately. With hearts of gratitude we praise you in Jesus's name. Amen

208

Give us this day our daily bread. (Matthew 6:11 NKJV)

Our Father in Heaven, you have given us life today; although we do not know what provisions you have awaiting us. Father God, one thing we do know is that we can face this day with the confident assurance that you will provide for us our daily bread. Thank you, Father God, for all other additional blessings you have scheduled for us today. Thank You for our "Daily Bread", This we thankfully pray in Jesus's name. Amen

209

Praise the LORD, all you nations; extol him, all you peoples. For great is his love toward us, and the faithfulness of the LORD endures forever. Praise the LORD. (Psalm 117:1-2 NIV)

O Lord Mighty and Merciful, you are worthy to be praised. We thank you for the inexhaustible fount of love you have given us. Thank you that nothing can separate us from your irrepressible love. We pray this in the name of the Father, Son and Holy Spirit. Amen

Blessed is the man who makes the LORD his trust, who does not look to the proud, to those who turn aside to false gods. (Psalm 40:4 NIV)

Father God, we come to you in the name of Jesus. Father God we experience many trials and tribulations in this life, only because we do not turn our cares over to you. Father God, as the trials come, we look at them as being so large and overwhelming. LORD God, as of today help us to not come to you telling about how large our problems are– but help us tell our problems how large our God is. This we pray in Jesus's name. Amen

Better a patient man than a warrior, a man who controls his temper than one who takes a city. (Proverbs 16:32 NIV)

Lord, how often does your handmade servants allow their tempers to flare against one another? Lord, help us to control our tempers so we speak ill of no one and cause harm to no one. Help us to not exert initiatory aggression against another human being. Lord this is our prayer, in the name of the Father, son and Holy Spirit. Amen

Do not say to yourself, "My power and the might of my own hand have gotten me this wealth." (Deuteronomy 8:17 NRSV)

Heavenly Father, people wallow in weakness only because they refuse to accept the strength offered through Christ Our Savior. Lord help people to first be honest with themselves realizing that under their own strength they are frail and thereby fail. All we accomplish is through your will. Father God help us to know that our strength is nothing unless you empower it to succeed, for strength comes from you alone. Father God, this we pray in Jesus's name. Amen

213

I thank God through Jesus Christ our Lord. So then with the mind I myself serve the law of God; but with the flesh the law of sin. (Romans 7:25 KJV)

Lord God Heavenly Father, we children of men struggle daily with double mindedness. Father God, on the outside everything looks normal, but within the corridors of our minds we are challenged between good and evil, right, and wrong. Lord God help us to make the right decisions and embrace the way of life which was illustrated by Jesus Christ our Lord and Savior. Lord in your mercy, hear our prayer in Jesus's name. Amen

214

For Ezra had prepared his heart to seek the law of the LORD, and to do *it*, and to teach in Israel statutes and judgments. (Ezra 7:10 KJV)

Lord, commitment to you and to your word will be the innermost desire of the heart of all who love you. Lord, set our hearts to study and live out your word in our daily lives. Lord, as we do this, showcase us before others so that they too will want to commit to you alone–as they reject the ways of this world. This we pray in the name of the Father, Son and Holy Spirit. Amen

215

Through Silvanus, whom I consider a faithful brother, I have written this short letter to encourage you and to testify that this is the true grace of God. Stand fast in it. (1 Peter 5:12 NRSV)

Lord God Almighty, we thank you for the Amazing Grace you have given us through the sacrifice of our Lord and Savior Jesus Christ. In his name we pray. Amen

216

Thus I will bless You while I live; I will lift up my hands in Your name. (Psalm 63:4 NKJV)

O Lord our God who dwells throughout the universe, we see the manifestation of your handiwork in our daily surroundings. Lord we see the clouds and sky, sun and moon, trees and grass and the faces of all you have created, both man and animal alike. Lord, as we live give us the unction to praise you as we lift our hands heavenward. This we pray in Jesus's name. Amen

217

My little children, these things I write to you, so that you may not sin. And if anyone sins, we have an Advocate with the Father, Jesus Christ the righteous. (1 John 2:1 NKJV)

Father God in Heaven, we approach you in the name of Jesus who speaks in our defense for our sinful acts. Father we ask your forgiveness and help that we not repeatedly commit those acts which are sinful in nature. This we ask in Jesus's name. Amen

218

**The eyes of the LORD are on the righteous and his
ears are attentive to their cry; (Psalm 34:15 NIV)**

LORD God Almighty, you are righteous and through Christ Jesus we
are found righteous in your sight. LORD, because of the righteousness
you have afforded us through Christ Jesus, you, O God our Father
forever has his eyes upon us and is ever attentive to our prayers. We are
grateful that our cries are heard–and are allowed into your presence.
This we gratefully pray in Jesus's name. Amen

219

**God saw that the light was good, and he separated
the light from the darkness. (Genesis 1:4 NIV)**

LORD God our Heavenly Father, we come to you in the name of
Jesus. You, O God have established order in the universe. You set
the heavens in motion. LORD, you separated the water from the
land and light from the darkness. Father God, you have given us an
example of order which eliminates chaos and promotes harmony.
Help us to use this insight while we are living on this earth to also
promote concord in our earthly existence. This we pray in Jesus's
name. Amen

220

**Sing to the LORD, praise his name; proclaim his
salvation day after day. (Psalm 96:2 NIV)**

O Lord our God, your name is Holy. Lord your name, "IAM", speaks
of your provision towards us your handmade servants. Lord we sing
praises to your name and worship you as our Savior. This we pray in
the name of the Father, Son and Holy Spirit. Amen

**I am astonished that you are so quickly deserting
the one who called you by the grace of Christ and
are turning to a different gospel. (Galatians 1:6 NIV)**

O God our Father, many are quick to say I am a Christian. Lord there comes a time in the life of your people as they profess Christ as Lord and savior saying, they choose to follow his will and his way. Later Lord they backslide and with unrepentant hearts remain immersed in worldly ways. Lord, help us all who vow and confess Christ as Savior the ability to remain true to the vow–so that you may take pleasure in them. This we ask in the matchless name of Jesus. Amen

**And the God of all grace, who called you to his
eternal glory in Christ, after you have suffered a
little while, will himself restore you and make you
strong, firm and steadfast. (1 Peter 5:10 NIV)**

Holy God of Grace, you have called your people to your eternal glory through Christ Jesus. Father God, we know that while we now go through menial sufferings there is a time of restoration ahead. We thank you for your plan of salvation which includes us your chosen people. This we pray in Jesus's name. Amen

**They were also to stand every morning to thank
and praise the LORD. They were to do the same in
the evening. (1 Chronicles 23:30 NIV)**

Good Morning Lord, thank you for watching over us as we slumbered last evening. Lord, please guide our thoughts today. Guide our walk today and guide our talk today. We thank you for watching over us until we slumber again this night. Lord forgive us our sins and keep us from evil. We pray this in the name of the Father, son, and Holy Spirit. Amen

224

When Jesus heard what had happened, he withdrew by boat privately to a solitary place. Hearing of this, the crowds followed him on foot from the towns. (Matthew 14:13 NIV)

Lord Jesus, we see your example of going off alone to a place of solitude, that we may seek the face of the Father as we offer heartfelt prayer. Lord, help us to seek this quiet time of revitalization as we recharge through spending time alone with the source of all power. This we pray in the name of the Father, Son and Holy Spirit. Amen

225

He has told you, O mortal, what is good; and what does the LORD require of you but to do justice, and to love kindness, and to walk humbly with your God? (Micah 6:8 NRSV)

O God, our Father in Heaven. Help us to walk humbly with you, love mercy and have a forgiving heart. This we pray in Jesus's name. Amen

226

he will sit as a refiner and purifier of silver, and he will purify the descendants of Levi and refine them like gold and silver, until they present offerings to the LORD in righteousness. (Malachi 3:3 NRSV)

O Lord our God, you are the Holy and Merciful refiner. Lord, turn up the heat and purify us until the dross of our lives and all contamination is removed, so that when you look at us you will see your face. Lord, we stand in agreement asking this in Jesus's name. Amen

227

My mouth shall speak wisdom; the meditation of my heart shall be understanding. (Psalm 49:3 ESV)

Lord God our Heavenly Father, life often tosses us challenges which are difficult to solve. You O God give us wisdom to solve what seems to be the unsolvable. Lord the wisdom you bestow gives us a heart of understanding, which is beneficial to the world around us. Thank you in Jesus's name. Amen

228

For our light and momentary troubles are achieving for us an eternal glory that far outweighs them all. (2 Corinthians 4:17 NIV)

O Lord our God, difficulties come, and difficulties go. Lord while we go through the struggles of life it is hard to understand the why of it all. One thing we followers of Christ do know, is that in the scheme of things as Christians those earthly troubles diminish in the light of the eternal promise we have through Jesus. Because of Christ Jesus we have grateful hearts. In his name we pray. Amen

229

"Blessed *is* the man who trusts in the LORD, And whose hope is the LORD. (Jeremiah 17:7 NKJV)

Our Father in Heaven, thank you for the blessings which come as a result of our trust in you–through Christ Jesus our redeemer. Our confidence is in Christ alone and it is through him we pray. Amen

230

O LORD, my strength and my fortress, my refuge in time of distress, to you the nations will come from the ends of the earth and say, "Our fathers possessed nothing but false gods, worthless idols that did them no good. (Jeremiah 16:19 NIV)

Lord God our creator, you have made mankind in your image, yet we openly walk in selfish pride. You, O God are the God who forgives the sins of pride and boasting. Please, Lord keep us from idolatry. You are the God who is our strength, fortification, and refuge during suffering. You, O God are the God who loves us beyond all that is known. You, O God are our Lord and our God. Hear our prayer as we pray in Jesus's name. Amen

231

Better the little that the righteous have than the wealth of many wicked; (Psalm 37:16 NIV)

O God, many people seek after the assets of this world. Father God, people lean towards undermining others as they seek after prestige, power, privilege, and wealth. Father God it is better to have contentment with enough than to seek after treasure which rusts and fades. Help us O God to find satisfaction in you and your provision while we are on this side of eternity. We pray this in Jesus's name. Amen

232

"Only take heed to yourself, and diligently keep yourself, lest you forget the things your eyes have seen, and lest they depart from your heart all the days of your life. And teach them to your children and your grandchildren, (Deuteronomy 4:9 NKJV)

Father God in Heaven, we children of men go through much in our lives. Many things happen yet how often do we forget your hands touching our lives. Father, we see the misdeeds of others yet forget our own. Father, we focus on the hardships we endure yet forget the comfort and peace you provide. Lord God our Heavenly Father, help us not forget the blessings you have given, etch them in our hearts. This we pray in Jesus's precious name. Amen

233

I said, "I will guard my ways that I may not sin with my tongue; I will keep a muzzle on my mouth as long as the wicked are in my presence." (Psalm 39:1 NRSV)

God of Compassion help us to guard our ways that we do not sin with our tongue. Lord, keep our words positive and supportive rather than insensitive and harmful. Help us be better. This we pray in Jesus's name. Amen

234

For the message of the cross is foolishness to those who are perishing, but to us who are being saved it is the power of God. (1 Corinthians 1:18 NIV)

Our Father in Heaven, we see the cross around us in many settings. People wear the cross as a piece of decorative jewelry around their necks or on bracelets on their arms, even on rings for their fingers. LORD to many it is just that, a piece of jewelry. For many LORD–it is a continual reminder of the sacrifice of Christ Jesus, who shed his blood for the benefit of all mankind. O God instill in the hearts of all people the understanding of your power Father God and how you used the cross to bring life. This we pray in Jesus's name. Amen

235

But just as he who called you is holy, so be holy in all you do. (1 Peter 1:15 NIV)

Lord God Almighty, you have called your people to be Holy. Help us O God to act in all things in a Holy manner that we may glorify you as our Holy and Loving God. Father God we ask that you hear our prayer in Jesus's name. Amen

236

Though the fig tree does not bud and there are no grapes on the vines, though the olive crop fails and the fields produce no food, though there are no sheep in the pen and no cattle in the stalls, yet I will rejoice in the LORD, I will be joyful in God my Savior. (Habakkuk 3:17-18 NIV)

Sovereign Lord God our Father, there are times when life is like a barren land–devoid of any good thing. We develop disease, relationships breakup, we experience lack of necessary resources and yes death takes our loved ones away. Lord, yet we will rejoice in you, we will be joyful in Christ Jesus our Savior who places joy in our hearts. Help us to walk in your delight daily Amen.

237

The great day of the LORD *is* near; *It is* near and hastens quickly. The noise of the day of the LORD is bitter; There the mighty men shall cry out. (Zephaniah 1:14 NKJV)

Lord, people place their hope in things which will not save them, silver and gold, accomplishments, and administrative authority. Lord, help those to know that it is only through the blood you shed that mankind can find salvation. Lord, help us to share this victorious message with those who do not know. We pray in the name of the Father, Son and Holy Spirit. Amen

238

When your words came, I ate them; they were my joy and my heart's delight, for I bear your name, O LORD God Almighty. (Jeremiah 15:16 NIV)

O LORD God Almighty, we voraciously devour your words because they give us life. Engage our hearts LORD to share the good news of your word with those who do not know it. LORD, hear our prayer in Jesus's name. Amen

239

Do not be overcome by evil, but overcome evil with good. (Romans 12:21 NIV)

Lord God of all that is right and good, show us how to not return evil for evil, but how to overcome evil with the good which dwells within our hearts, which come from our Lord Jesus Christ. We pray this in the name of the Father, Son and Holy Spirit. Amen

240

The commandments, "Do not commit adultery," "Do not murder," "Do not steal," "Do not covet," and whatever other commandment there may be, are summed up in this one rule: "Love your neighbor as yourself." (Romans 13:9 NIV)

Lord help us to love one another as you have loved us. This we pray in Jesus's holy and precious name. Amen

241

Whoever gives heed to instruction prospers, and blessed is he who trusts in the LORD. (Proverbs 16:20 NIV)

Lord God Almighty, we hear the word prosper and we immediately think of riches. Lord, the only true prosperity comes through having a relationship with you through our Lord and Savior Jesus Christ. Lord God, through the salvation you brought to the earth we have everlasting riches stored up for us in eternity. Help all people to know and understand this spiritual prosperity. This we pray in Jesus's name. Amen

242

And lead us not into temptation, but deliver us from evil: For thine is the kingdom, and the power, and the glory, forever. Amen. (Matthew 6:13 KJV)

Our Father in Heaven, we place our hand in your hand as you lead us through each day. Father God, we can trust with complete confidence that you will allow only your will in our lives—if we just wholly place our confidence in you. We in our own strength do not know the way to go, but your leading us along life's pathways get us through the crooked places and over the rough places. Thank you that we can trust where you lead us. Lord, in your mercy hear our prayer. Amen

243

As thou knowest not what *is* the way of the spirit, *nor* how the bones *do grow* in the womb of her that is with child: even so thou knowest not the works of God who maketh all. (Ecclesiastes 11:5 KJV)

Lord God our creator, we children of men know nothing of the path of the breath of life. LORD we know less of how the body is formed in the womb of a mother. O God we do not understand many of the things you have placed in motion on this earth. Father God there is one thing we do know above all else, you love us with an unyielding love. Thank you from the bottom of our hearts as we pray in Jesus's name. Amen

244

I do not set aside the grace of God; for if righteousness *comes* through the law, then Christ died in vain." (Galatians 2:21 NKJV)

Father God help us to not make a mockery of the cross by setting aside the Grace you have so freely given through the death of Christ Jesus. Enable all people to understand that we cannot receive Salvation through the works of our flesh. Lord, in your mercy hear our prayer. Amen

245

For who has despised the day of small things? For these seven rejoice to see The plumb line in the hand of Zerubbabel. They are the eyes of the LORD, Which scan to and fro throughout the whole earth." (Zechariah 4:10 NKJV)

Lord God Almighty, we look at the situations around us and feel that we can make little difference if any at all. Yet Lord if we are faithful enough to begin the process, you are mighty enough to bring it to completion. Help us to be faithful planters of the seed of change for the betterment of this world. This we pray in Jesus's name. Amen

246

I spread out my hands to You; My soul *longs* for You like a thirsty land. Selah (Psalm 143:6 NKJV)

Father God in Heaven, we lift our hands to you as a child reaching out to hold the hand of its parent. We need you O God for we can do nothing without you. O God help us to never forget this as we travel through the arid land called life. We pray in Jesus's name. Amen

247

Be joyful in hope, patient in affliction, faithful in prayer. (Romans 12:12 NIV)

Lord God Heavenly Father, there is much discord, deception, and disdain in this life we children of men experience. But Father–despite the afflictions, despite the let downs we place our hope in Christ Jesus. It is through Christ we seek patience as we pass through the afflictions. It is through Christ that we receive our strength. It is through Christ that we can faithfully pray. It is through Christ Jesus that we pray this prayer. Amen

248

"Do not keep talking so proudly or let your mouth speak such arrogance, for the LORD is a God who knows, and by him deeds are weighed. (1 Samuel 2:3 NIV)

O God, our LORD, you know what dwells in the hearts of people. LORD, you see the mouth which speaks arrogantly and proudly, which is filled with lies. For out of the mouth proceeds the abundance of the heart. O God, for mercy's sake help your people cleanse their hearts. LORD God, we ask forgiveness for our sinful actions because we know in fact that our deeds will one day be weighed by you. Lord in your mercy, hear our prayer. Amen

249

When the poor and needy seek water, and there is none, and their tongue is parched with thirst, I the LORD will answer them, I the God of Israel will not forsake them. (Isaiah 41:17 NRSV)

Father God, you know intimately the faces and hearts of your people throughout the world. Father God people seek out their needs, as a parched person searches for water to quench their thirst. Although people seem challenged to the point of not receiving necessary resources, you speak provision into the lives of those who trust you, they hear you saying. But I the LORD will answer them; I, the God of Israel, will not forsake them. We thank you in Jesus's name that we can rest in the assurance that you know our every need and that you are our Jehovah Jireh our provider. Amen

250

Be completely humble and gentle; be patient, bearing with one another in love. (Ephesians 4:2 NIV)

Gracious and Loving Lord God, we see as an example the life of our Lord and Savior Jesus Christ how to live a humble, gentle, and patient life. O God our creator please help us in the fullness of your divine Trinity to live at peace and with love towards one another. This we pray in the name of the Father, Son and Holy Spirit. Amen

251

By this everyone will know that you are my disciples, if you have love for one another." (John 13:35 NRSV)

God of love, you are love. O God, you alone can change the hearts and minds of the people on this earth. Help us O God to not act out of selfishness and empty conceit, bias, and prejudice. Father God how can we say we love you whom we have not seen when we do not love one another who we see daily? Father God, help us and forgive us, lead us, and guide us so that the relationships of this world reflect how it will one day be in the New Jerusalem. This we pray in Jesus's Holy name. Amen

252

"Whoever acknowledges me before men, I will also acknowledge him before my Father in heaven. (Matthew 10:32 NIV)

Lord Jesus, through your Holy Spirit help all mankind to confess you before this world, so that in due time you will confess us all before God our Father in Heaven. Amen

253

What then? shall we sin, because we are not under the law, but under grace? God forbid. (Romans 6:15 KJV)

Father God in Heaven, sin is ever knocking at the door of our lives. Father God, as we seek to stand behind the cross of Christ Jesus as protection, please keep Satan and his demons at bay that we do not fall into the seductive temptations of sin. Lord in your mercy; hear our prayer as we pray it in Jesus's name. Amen

254

A sound heart *is* life to the body, But envy *is* rottenness to the bones. (Proverbs 14:30 NKJV)

Lord God our Heavenly Father, many times in the lives of your people they cannot and will not rejoice in the praise of others because of envy. Lord envy can cause people to lie, cheat, steal and kill to make sure the thing they want is not enjoyed by another. Lord, give us peace and unity in Christ Jesus. Enable us to appreciate what you have placed in our lives; in the lives of others and that our collective bodies receive life through your blessed grace. This is our prayer in Jesus's name. Amen

255

For one believes with the heart and so is justified, and one confesses with the mouth and so is saved. (Romans 10:10 NRSV)

Lord God heavenly Father, we thank you for the salvation earned for us by Jesus's death on the cross and his resurrection from the dead. Lord, by the power of the Holy Spirit help us to confess this good news to all who would listen. Thank you for the heart of belief you have given us which justifies and the mouth which confesses Christ as Lord. We pray this in the name of the Father, Son and Holy Spirit. Amen

256

Beloved, now we are children of God; and it has not yet been revealed what we shall be, but we know that when He is revealed, we shall be like Him, for we shall see Him as He is. (1 John 3:2 NKJV)

Father God, we your children are now clothed in these earthly bodies which deteriorate as the years advance. Thank you, Father God for the hope which is given us through Christ Jesus. We understand that through Jesus we are called your children and that one day we shall see you just as you are, and we shall be like Him in our new spiritual bodies. What a wonderful future you have prepared for us as we walk towards eternity, thank you. Through Christ Jesus we pray. Amen

257

The righteous cry out, and the LORD hears them; he delivers them from all their troubles. (Psalm 34:17 NIV)

Our Father in Heaven, through Christ Jesus the righteous cry out during their encounter with trouble and you deliver them. Thank you, Lord Jesus. Amen

258

He who did not spare his own Son, but gave him up for us all--how will he not also, along with him, graciously give us all things? (Romans 8:32 NIV)

Lord God of Grace, you chose to not spare Jesus Christ your son from the suffering and death on the cross; through Him we your hand made servants have received redemption. Lord God, if you go that far to provide eternal life which is the most important thing that a human being can receive from you. Then surely the less important things of this life you will also give according to your will. We thank you in Jesus's name. Amen

259

Whoever watches the wind will not plant; whoever looks at the clouds will not reap. (Ecclesiastes 11:4 NIV)

God of Grace, we your created people often miss opportunities because we are looking for the ideal time to act. Lord God, regardless of how things around us may look, help us to step out in faith that you may work on our behalf. Lord God strengthen our faith walk daily. This we pray in Jesus's name. Amen

260

Let no one say when he is tempted, "I am tempted by God"; for God cannot be tempted by evil, nor does He Himself tempt anyone. (James 1:13 NKJV)

Father God in Heaven, we are often tempted by many things in this life. Father, we are tempted by the lust of the flesh, lust of the eyes and other ungodly evil desires which we can so easily fall victim to. Father God, as Christ Jesus was able to overcome temptation in the wilderness, help us to do so daily as these desires of the flesh are presented to us. Strengthen us so that we may glorify you in our avoidance of them. Lord in your mercy; hear our prayer as we pray through Christ Jesus our Lord and Savior. Amen

261

He who walks with wise *men* will be wise, But the companion of fools will be destroyed. (Proverbs 13:20 NKJV)

Lord God our exalted Teacher, teach us to unite with wise people that we ourselves may grow wise. Lord, association brings on assimilation. We your children desire incorporation into your realm of wisdom not the earthly realm of irrationality. We pray this in the name of the Father, Son and Holy Spirit. Amen

262

Let the morning bring me word of your unfailing love, for I have put my trust in you. Show me the way I should go, for to you I lift up my soul. (Psalm 143:8 NIV)

O God our Lord, each new day brings with it new challenges. Lord God, as we begin a new day, motivate our hearts to seek your unfailing love– to strengthen us as we place our trust in you for all things. Lord God show us the path to follow each day. This is our prayer in Jesus's name. Amen

263

so that from the rising of the sun to the place of its setting men may know there is none besides me. I am the LORD, and there is no other. (Isaiah 45:6 NIV)

O Lord our God–from the rising of the sun through the setting of the same you watch over your children. Lord God, as the sun courses through the daytime sky and the moon courses through the nighttime sky you watch over your children. Thank you, Lord God for always keeping watch over us like the Good Shepherd you are. We offer our thank you in Jesus's name. Amen

264

Wisdom *is* the principal thing; *Therefore* get wisdom. And in all your getting, get understanding. (Proverbs 4:7 NKJV)

Dear Lord God, as we continue in our Christian walk, enable us to seek above all else wisdom. Lord though it cost us everything help us to get understanding. Lord God, this is our supreme goal which goes hand in hand with placing our faith in Christ as our Lord and Savior. Lord in your mercy, hear our prayer. Amen

265

He gives power to the faint, and strengthens the powerless. (Isaiah 40:29 NRSV)

Lord God Almighty, We children of men are challenged with the struggles of life. Lord, those struggles often leave us battered and exhausted. Lord we saw our Lord Jesus Christ walk through the struggle of moving towards the cross of Calvary with the power you gave him. Lord God, likewise, give us power to continue in daily life while the blood runs warm in our veins–that we may glorify you in all that we do. This is our prayer in Jesus's name. Amen

266

"Who has ever given to God, that God should repay him?" (Romans 11:35 NIV)

O God our Father, we can never give you anything to repay all you have done in our lives. Father God accept our meager offering of praise and worship as our means of thanks not as recompense. Lord in your mercy, hear our prayer. Amen

267

For where two or three are gathered together in My name, I am there in the midst of them." (Matthew 18:20 NKJV)

Lord Jesus, we stand in agreement on the power of your name that we want to follow you and be more Christ like in all we say, think and do. We know you are with us in this pursuit, as in your word it is written that where two or more come together in your name you are there. Guide us we pray. Amen

268

See that no one renders evil for evil to anyone, but always pursue what is good both for yourselves and for all. (1 Thessalonians 5:15 NKJV)

Lord, life offers many opportunities where we could return evil for evil. Lord, that is not your way of doing things nor should it be our way.

Lord, allow kindness to blossom in our hearts that we might be kind to one another rather than cruel and heartless. Help us to live out the second greatest commandment to love one another. This we pray in the name of the Father, Son and Holy Spirit. Amen

269

Devote yourselves to prayer, keeping alert in it with thanksgiving. (Colossians 4:2 NRSV)

Lord God, our heavenly Father–help us to pray often and continually so we may be able to draw strength from being in your presence. This we pray in Jesus's name. Amen

270

that you may approve the things that are excellent, that you may be sincere and without offense till the day of Christ, (Philippians 1:10 NKJV)

O God, we come to you in the name of Jesus with lifted, opened hands asking your forgiveness for failing in our Christian walk. O God–give us a spirit of discernment that before we slip, we are made aware of the incident so we can prayerfully seek to avoid taking any wrong action. Lord in your mercy, hear our prayer. Amen

271

When Christ who is your life appears, then you also will appear with him in glory. (Colossians 3:4 ESV)

Lord Jesus, we look forward to the day you will return because we know that on that day you will take us home to be with you in Glory. We thank you for being our atoning sacrifice which brought us into right relationship with God the Father. Amen

272

Therefore, prepare your minds for action; be self-controlled; set your hope fully on the grace to be given you when Jesus Christ is revealed. (1 Peter 1:13 NIV)

LORD God our Father, guide and perfect our minds that we maintain correct thinking and discharge the duties which bring you glory as we continue our Christian walk. In Jesus's name we pray. Amen

273

See what love the Father has given us, that we should be called children of God; and that is what we are. The reason the world does not know us is that it did not know him. (1 John 3:1 NRSV)

Lord God our Heavenly Father, you love us with an unconditional love beyond comparison. Father God your unconditional love does not equate to unconditional approval of sinful actions. Thank you that you love us even when we fall and fail to live according to your will for our lives. Thank you for allowing us to be called "Children of God". Thank you for Jesus who has brought us back into right relationship with you. It is in Jesus's name we pray. Amen

274

Then he said to them all: "If anyone would come after me, he must deny himself and take up his cross daily and follow me. (Luke 9:23 NIV)

Lord Jesus we love you, we want to do whatever is required of us to follow you as you instruct us to. Lord, you endured the pain of the cross that we might be redeemed and have the right to eternal life.

Help us Lord Jesus to daily bear our cross as we make every effort to deny self and follow you. We ask this Lord Jesus so we may glorify God our Father. Amen

275

The eyes of all look to you, and you give them their food at the proper time. (Psalm 145:15 NIV)

El Shaddai – You are the All Sufficient, you give us all we need as we walk through life. O God forgive us when we think you are not meeting our needs. Although you may not answer in the way we think you ought, your answer is in the way that is best for us. We offer gratitude for the greatest provision of all, salvation through Christ Jesus. If you never give us anything else, you have already done enough. O God our provider, hear our prayer as we pray in Jesus's name. Amen

276

When Jesus spoke again to the people, he said, "I am the light of the world. Whoever follows me will never walk in darkness, but will have the light of life." (John 8:12 NIV)

Lord Jesus, there are times in our lives when darkness attempts to overtake us, blinding us, then impeding our progress. Lord, it is at those times that the light of your word illuminates the darkness– enabling us to make it through those situations. Lord, your word is a light for our feet and a lamp for our path as we take our steps through life. Your word Lord removes the uncertainty of the darkness as our path is brightened and visible. Help us Lord Jesus to follow you as our daily light. Amen

277

Now, therefore, you are no longer strangers and foreigners, but fellow citizens with the saints and members of the household of God. (Ephesians 2:19 NKJV)

Lord God Almighty, through Christ Jesus we are no longer aliens and foreigners to you–now we are considered as members of your household. Thank you, Lord, for citizenship which we will one day rejoice in and come to experience when we come into that prepared place you have awaiting us. We pray in Jesus's name. Amen

278

'For in him we live and move and have our being.' As some of your own poets have said, 'We are his offspring.'

Lord, you gave mankind life and through you we live, move, and have our being. We exist, only because of you. We thank you that you have allowed us to be at this time and in this place. Our prayer is that we glorify you in all we say, think and do. Help us Lord to achieve this goal. We implore you in Jesus's name. Amen

279

Nevertheless do not rejoice in this, that the spirits are subject to you, but rather rejoice because your names are written in heaven." (Luke 10:20 NKJV)

Father God, we come to you in the name of Jesus thanking you that our names are written in Heaven, because of His sacrifice to make it so. There is nothing more we need or can ask for. Amen

280

Since we have now been justified by his blood, how much more shall we be saved from God's wrath through him! (Romans 5:9 NIV)

Lord Jesus, it is through your shed blood that we are now justified and saved from the wrath of God and the eternal death. Thank you for doing for us what we could have never done for ourselves. In your name Lord. Amen

281

He said to them: "It is not for you to know the times or dates the Father has set by his own authority. (Acts 1:7 NIV)

Lord Jesus our Savior, we know that one day you will return to this world to carry home those who have placed their faith in you. Lord, through your Holy Spirit help us to share the message of salvation with those who do not yet know you, so they too may be saved to eternal life. Amen

282

For the wages of sin *is* death, but the gift of God *is* eternal life in Christ Jesus our Lord. (Romans 6:23 NKJV)

LORD God Heavenly Father, we thank you for the gift of salvation given through Christ Jesus. LORD, unlike the gifts we receive from family and friends we will not say "you shouldn't have". LORD, instead we say thank you, while we have the breath of life in our bodies. Thank you, LORD–as we dwell on this earth for giving us what we could not obtain for ourselves. LORD God, we pray this in Jesus's name. Amen

283

You are forgiving and good, O Lord, abounding in love to all who call to you. (Psalm 86:5 NIV)

O Lord our God, you abound in mercy. Lord, as we come confessing our sin you stand ready to forgive. Lord, you are good, forgiving and loving towards all who call upon your Holy name. Amen

284

You did not choose me but I chose you. And I appointed you to go and bear fruit, fruit that will last, so that the Father will give you whatever you ask him in my name. (John 15:16 NRSV)

Lord, it has been said by many "I found the Lord". Those who are aware know this is not true. Lord, you were never lost. You continually sought after us even in our ignorance. Lord, you have chosen us individually. Help us, your chosen people to bear fruit that will last and to offer to all around us the message of salvation, which demonstrates your love for all mankind. Lord in your mercy, hear our prayer. Amen

285

Every day I will bless You, And I will praise Your name forever and ever. (Psalm 145:2 NKJV)

Lord God Almighty you alone are great and worthy to be praised. Lord, please accept our heartfelt praise. Amen

286

"You are the light of the world. A city on a hill cannot be hidden. (Matthew 5:14 NIV)

Lord, as a light shines' in the darkness and that darkness is dispelled let our light shine. Lord, if our light dims because of spiritual disruption, please reconnect us back into the source which is you. Lord, allow us to always shine brightly as we give glory and honor to you. We pray this in the name of the Father, Son and Holy spirit. Amen

287

Therefore I praised the dead who were already dead, More than the living who are still alive. (Ecclesiastes 4:2 NKJV)

Lord, we live in a world full of pain and trouble. Lord, if not for what lies ahead, we children of men would have an existence of untold misery. But because you are our Salvation, we know that there are brighter days ahead. Thank you. Amen

288

Let us hear the conclusion of the whole matter: Fear God, and keep his commandments: for this _is_ the whole _duty_ of man. (Ecclesiastes 12:13 KJV)

Father God, some of us your created people–seek through the works of the hands to manipulate creation to cater to mankind's every whim. Father God, by people doing this they are in fact attempting to compete with you. Father God forgive the ignorance of mankind. Father God help mankind to understand that the whole duty of man is to be in awe of you and live by your commands. Father God hear our prayer in Jesus's name. Amen

289

But whosoever drinketh of the water that I shall give him shall never thirst; but the water that I shall

give him shall be in him a well of water springing up into everlasting life. (John 4:14 KJV)

Lord Jesus, We children of men allow the material things of this world to seduce us into thinking that through them we will find happiness. The truth is they never satisfy and always leave us with an empty feeling. Only you Lord, can quench the thirst we have. Lord help us to understand that as you quench our thirst, you are quenching our thirst for life. Eternal life is what we thirst for. Lord we thank you. Amen

290

Let each of you look out not only for his own interests, but also for the interests of others. (Philippians 2:4 NKJV)

Lord God Almighty, we come to a time of year when people are bustling about to obtain gifts for family and friends. Lord God–help us to remember the less fortunate in that season of giving. Lord God remove the miserly spirit and replace it with an altruistic spirit. This we pray in Jesus's name. Amen

291

Sometimes there is a way that seems to be right, but in the end it is the way to death. (Proverbs 16:25 NRSV)

Lord God Heavenly Father, there are many people who say there are many routes to you O God. Father God, we know from your word there is only one way and that is through "The Way", Jesus. Father help those who do not know that Jesus is the only way to eternal life. Father God help them to understand that there is no other way so that they do not experience the second death. This we pray in Jesus's name. Amen

292

I am Alpha and Omega, the beginning and the end, the first and the last. (Revelation 22:13 KJV)

Lord Jesus you are in total control of the outcome of this world because you are its creator. Lord Jesus, you are the beginning and you are the end of all that was, is and ever shall be. We praise your Holy Name. Amen

293

Jesus answered and said to them, "This is the work of God, that you believe in Him whom He sent." (John 6:29 NKJV)

Father God, above all else help us to believe in Christ Jesus our Lord and Savior. In Jesus's name we pray. Amen

294

Be of good courage, And He shall strengthen your heart, All you who hope in the LORD. (Psalm 31:24 NKJV)

Precious Lord, you gave up your home in Heaven to take on human flesh and live among us, to be born like us, cry like us, hunger like us, tire like us, thirst like us and die like us, so that you could redeem us. Thank you, Lord Jesus, thank you. Amen

295

Glory to God in the highest, and on earth peace, good will toward men. (Luke 2:14 KJV)

Lord God, this speaks to a season of peace and harmony. Many people are more congenial at this time of year than others. Help us Father God to remain so during the ensuing year. This we pray in Jesus's name. Amen

296

You will show me the path of life; In Your presence *is* fullness of joy; At Your right hand *are* pleasures forevermore. (Psalm 16:11 NKJV)

Gracious Loving and Eternal Father God, you have placed joy down in the hearts of those who know you through your son Christ Jesus. You direct our path through life, and we find joy in the simple things you have given for our pleasure. Because of Jesus, we know that although we find enjoyment in the menial things here on earth, we will one day find immeasurable joy in your presence in that place Christ has prepared for us. In Jesus's name we ask that you receive this prayer. Amen

297

and the peace of God, which surpasses all understanding, will guard your hearts and minds through Christ Jesus. (Philippians 4:7 NKJV)

Lord Jesus, you alone offer us the peace that surpasses all understanding. Through your shed blood we now have peace with God the Father, which assures our hope of the future you have awaiting us. Help us Lord Jesus to make known that same peace is available to all our brothers and sisters on earth. Amen

298

He will keep you strong to the end, so that you will be blameless on the day of our Lord Jesus Christ. (1 Corinthians 1:8 NIV)

Father God, we approach you in the name of Jesus. As we move towards the end of each year, we know there is another end yet to come, if you allow us to see it. Lord Jesus by your spirit, help us to solely rely on you to be blameless on the day of your return–to gather those who are yours. Holy Spirit show us how to remain faithful and true as we await the day. We pray in the name of the Father, Son and Holy Spirit. Amen

299

He has put a new song in my mouth-- Praise to our God; Many will see *it* and fear And will trust in the LORD. (Psalm 40:3 NKJV)

LORD God Heavenly Father, you have given us the opportunity to see new sun rises and sunsets. LORD, you put a new song of joy in our mouths and hearts through the love you constantly demonstrate in our lives. LORD, we praise you for carrying us this far in life and for sending us Christ to carry us into life eternal. Through Christ Jesus we pray. Amen

300

'Sir,' the man replied, 'leave it alone for one more year, and I'll dig around it and fertilize it. (Luke 13:8 NIV)

Gracious Lord, it is very possible that in preceding times we were not as productive as we should have or could have been. Lord, impregnate us with your Word that we become productive beyond the point of abundance. Help us Lord to be inexhaustible in our participation as your hands, eyes, ears, voice, and feet in the building of your kingdom here on earth. Lord, help us to recognize that each new day given is a day we should use for accomplishing your work in the kingdom while we still have breath. Lord, we ask you the hear our prayer. Amen

Therefore he is able to save completely those who come to God through him, because he always lives to intercede for them. (Hebrews 7:25 NIV)

Lord Jesus our Priestly representative, you intercede for us before the Father asking that we be saved despite of our continual failings. Lord Jesus, you save completely and permanently. You are our High Priest forever, thank you. Amen

Therefore, to him who knows to do good and does not do *it,* to him it is sin. (James 4:17 NKJV)

LORD God, we your handmade servants are instilled with the knowledge to discern between right and wrong. LORD, we often allow the world to have its way and direct the actions of our lives. LORD, forgive us for knowing better yet not doing better, how wretched we are even in our own eyes. LORD, help us to not fall into worldly ways but to walk in your ways. Forgive us LORD because we do not want to sin, but sin is there coaxing, manipulating, and sticking to us like a magnet. Thank you for forgiving us because of Christ Jesus when we fall short. Through Jesus we pray. Amen

Therefore, since the promise of entering his rest still stands, let us be careful that none of you be found to have fallen short of it. (Hebrews 4:1 NIV)

Lord Jesus, your promise of rest stands forever to those who will accept it. Although through you Lord, we receive a temporary rest in this life which affords us a future hope, we look forward to the life to come.

Lord, in you the day is coming when we will have eternal rest from the contamination of sin. Thank you, Lord Jesus. Amen

302

Where can I go from your Spirit? Where can I flee from your presence? (Psalm 139:7 NIV)

Lord God Heavenly Father, we thank you for another new day. Father God, although we do not know what lies ahead in this day, we know you do and therefore we can move ahead in confidence that you will be there in the midst of wherever we find ourselves. Thank you for your loving care. This we pray in Jesus's name. Amen

303

After this manner therefore pray ye: Our Father which art in heaven, Hallowed be thy name. (Matthew 6:9 KJV)

LORD God our Heavenly Father. You created us and through you we are fearfully and wonderfully made. Yet LORD, more than just our creator you are our Father. You, Father God give warmth, compassion, security, protection, and provision. You Father, our Sacred God who sent your son as the incarnate God to die for our sins—so we could be found acceptable through Him. Thank you, Father God. In Jesus's name we pray. Amen

304

As you do not know what *is* the way of the wind, *Or* how the bones *grow* in the womb of her who is with child, So you do not know the works of God who makes everything. (Ecclesiastes 11:5 NKJV)

Most Gracious and Omniscient Father God, while we your children are living on this earth, we can never truly discern the reasoning behind your works. But one thing Father is true we can trust you to know what is best for all your creation. Thank you in Jesus's name. Amen

305

Your mercy, O LORD, *is* in the heavens; Your faithfulness *reaches* to the clouds. (Psalm 36:5 NKJV)

O Lord, your steadfast love reaches to the heavens and your faithfulness never fails. Lord, help our love for one another to reach as far. Amen

306

"But what about you?" he asked. "Who do you say I am?" Peter answered, "The Christ of God." (Luke 9:20 NIV)

Lord Jesus, you asked the disciples, "who do you say I am"; Peter replied that you are the Christ of God. Thank you, Lord for being our salvation, thank you for taking our sins to the cross, thank you for rising from the dead which illustrates that one day we too will rise to be with you in Glory. Thank you, our Messiah. Amen

307

For God was pleased to have all his fullness dwell in him, and through him to reconcile to himself all things, whether things on earth or things in heaven, by making peace through his blood, shed on the cross. (Colossians 1:19-20 NIV)

Lord Jesus, the only peace we have comes through you. You, O Lord secured our peace with God the Father by shedding your precious blood on the cross of Calvary. Lord, let your peace rule in this world that mankind may act in a civil manner one to another. Amen

308

But for that very reason I was shown mercy so that in me, the worst of sinners, Christ Jesus might display his unlimited patience as an example for those who would believe on him and receive eternal life. (1 Timothy 1:16 NIV)

O God our Heavenly Father, you have been exceedingly patient with us your children. Father God, you are slow to anger and longsuffering where we are concerned. This is the attitude we should have towards one another. LORD, you had put up with all the wickedness of mankind and then you sent Christ to bring us back into right relationship with you. How wonderful is your patience, your grace and your mercy, towards your hand made servants. Thank you always in Jesus's name. Amen

309

But we see Jesus, who was made a little lower than the angels, now crowned with glory and honor because he suffered death, so that by the grace of God he might taste death for everyone. (Hebrews 2:9 NIV)

Lord Jesus–because you took on human flesh you were a little lower than the angels. Although you were clothed in human flesh you never sinned. Lord because you never sinned, you were able to be our sin offering, and for that you are crowned with glory. Thank you for tasting death for everyone that we might receive eternal life. Lord in your Mercy hear our prayer. Amen

310

For this God *is* our God for ever and ever: he will be our guide *even* unto death. (Psalm 48:14 KJV)

Father God, you are our God forever and ever. There are some who yet do not know you through Christ our redeeming Savior. Father God show us who, when and where to share the message of salvation which is found in Christ Jesus. Make us eager ambassadors of your word. This is our prayer. We pray in the name of the Father, Son and Holy Spirit. Amen

311

You will keep *him* in perfect peace, *Whose* mind *is* stayed *on You,* Because he trusts in You. (Isaiah 26:3 NKJV)

Heavenly Father God, we go through many trials and tribulations. Each new day presents new challenges. Father God, some of those challenges confound and overwhelm us. But LORD when we take our minds off those things and place our minds on you, you give us perfect peace. Thank you that we can trust you through Christ for the peace of the eternal hope of a brighter future. Amen

312

Let your gentleness be evident to all. The Lord is near. (Philippians 4:5 NIV)

Dear Heavenly Father–help us to be gentle in all situations so that everyone we meet experience your closeness through us. This is our prayer through Christ our Savior. Amen

313

This righteousness from God comes through faith in Jesus Christ to all who believe. There is no difference, (Romans 3:22 NIV)

Father God, you made Christ Jesus who knew no sin to be sin for us, so that in him we might become the righteous people you intended us to be. Father God we can never ever thank you enough. In Jesus's name we pray. Amen

314

For the grace of God that brings salvation has appeared to all men. (Titus 2:11 NIV)

Lord Jesus, it is only because you have come into the world bringing salvation that our once troubled conscience can now peacefully know that we are not lost to eternity. Help us to teach this truth to all mankind. In the Name of the Father, Son and the Holy Spirit. Amen

315

She gave this name to the LORD who spoke to her: "You are the God who sees me," for she said, "I have now seen the One who sees me." (Genesis 16:13 NIV)

O LORD our God, you are the God who sees our every move. From the rising of the sun to the setting of the same you watch over your children, seeing our every move. O LORD we see you also in the faces of the passerby who offer a smile and in the gleam in the eye of a friend or loved one. We love you LORD, but you first loved us by offering Christ to give us eternal life. Amen

316

In your struggle against sin, you have not yet resisted to the point of shedding your blood. (Hebrews 12:4 NIV)

Lord Jesus, we children of men struggle against sin constantly. Lord Jesus we sin in thought, word, and deed. Thank you for being the Sacrificial Lamb whose blood was shed to redeem us. Help us live worthy of the wonderful gift you have given. Amen

317

Turn away my eyes from looking at worthless things, and revive me in Your way. (Psalm 119:37 NKJV)

Eternal Father God, you see all things past, present, and future. Lord turn our eyes away from that, which will not benefit, edify, improve, or sanctify us. This is our prayer in Jesus's name. Amen

318

Fight the good fight of the faith. Take hold of the eternal life to which you were called when you made your good confession in the presence of many witnesses. (1 Timothy 6:12 NIV)

LORD God our Heavenly Father, within the strength given us we faithfully take hold of the eternal life offered through Christ Jesus. Father God help us to continually fight the good fight of faith as we boldly stand before the world confessing Christ and Him–crucified for our salvation. In the name of Jesus, we pray. Amen

319

We know that anyone born of God does not continue to sin; the one who was born of God keeps him safe, and the evil one cannot harm him. (1 John 5:18 NIV)

Dear Lord Jesus, we children of men being reborn to God the Father through Baptism, earnestly seek to be rid of sin. Lord Jesus, we thank you who was born of God as you keep us safe from the evil one. Amen

320

There is neither Jew nor Greek, there is neither slave nor free, there is neither male nor female; for you are all one in Christ Jesus. (Galatians 3:28 NKJV)

Gracious Father God, we come to you as humbly as we know how in the name of Jesus. Father God, as we observe one another we do not all look alike, communicate alike or worship alike. We are different in skin tones, hair color, eye color, language, customs, political views, gender, and ethnic origin. Father God despite the differences which cause separation we are all one as we place our faith in Christ Jesus as our one true Lord and Savior. Father God purge the division from among those who proclaim Christ as Lord. LORD God let your children live with peace, and in harmony as Christian love unites us into one living body of believers. This is our prayer which we pray in Jesus's name. Amen

321

Every good and perfect gift is from above, coming down from the Father of the heavenly lights, who does not change like shifting shadows. (James 1:17 NIV)

Dear God, our Father, how often do we your children focus on the negatives of life. LORD God, we so often miss the miracles you perform before our eyes because we fixate on the dreary, the broken, the difficult and the brokenness of this world. LORD, help us embrace the continued blessings of life you shower upon us daily. Thank you, LORD, for the many good gifts you continually give us. Thank you most of all for the salvation found in Jesus our Lord and Savior in whose name we pray. Amen

322

"Can you fathom the mysteries of God? Can you probe the limits of the Almighty? (Job 11:7 NIV)

Lord God our creator, you are farther above us than the heavens are above the earth. Lord we cannot always understand you and your ways, but we can always trust you. Thank you, Lord God, that you are not small enough to understand because if you were, then you would not be large enough to worship. We ask that you hear our prayer in Jesus's name. Amen

323

We proclaim to you what we have seen and heard, so that you also may have fellowship with us. And our fellowship is with the Father and with his Son, Jesus Christ. (1 John 1:3 NIV)

Lord Jesus, help us to remain in close relationship with you as we seek your presence in prayer, so that we can be conformed to your image. We desire above all else to have fellowship with God the Father, and with you, God the Son–and with God the Holy Spirit. Speak to our hearts Lord Jesus that we may know you more deeply each day and draw ever closer to you and your Holiness. Amen

324

But you, when you pray, go into your room, and when you have shut your door, pray to your Father who *is* in the secret *place;* and your Father who sees in secret will reward you openly. (Matthew 6:6 NKJV)

God of Grace, Glory and Strength, in our weakness we humbly approach you in the name of Jesus. Father God you see our dishonor and give us your grace. Father God you see us in our weakness and give us your strength. One day Father God we will see Jesus coming to carry us home from this wilderness to the Glory he has prepared for us, and all will see us receive our reward. In Jesus's name we thank you for everything and for hearing our prayers. Amen

325

For the LORD gives wisdom, and from his mouth come knowledge and understanding. (Proverbs 2:6 NIV)

Lord Jesus, other people are often eager and ready to give us counsel, but we must proceed cautiously with human advice. From you alone Lord, is true wisdom and knowledge found. When we rely on human understanding and advice alone often, we fail in our undertakings. Thank you, dear Lord Jesus for being the sole provider of wisdom and true knowledge for mankind. Lead us; guide us along our way Lord Jesus. Amen

326

Good and upright is the LORD; therefore he instructs sinners in his ways. (Psalm 25:8 NIV)

Lord God you are good all the time. Lord you teach sinners your ways, teach us Lord, teach us that we may live according to your will. In Jesus's name we offer our prayer. Amen

327

"Come, follow me," Jesus said, "and I will make you fishers of men." (Mark 1:17 NIV)

Lord Jesus as you spoke to your disciples "follow me", your words fall upon those today who claim you as savior. Help us Lord Jesus to follow you and as we do, we can then lead others to you so they too may become followers who lead others to you as we all follow your footsteps. Amen

328

There is one body and one Spirit-- just as you were called to one hope when you were called-- one Lord, one faith, one baptism; one God and Father of all, who is over all and through all and in all. (Ephesians 4:4-6 NIV)

O LORD we come in the name of Jesus. O LORD the people of this world are of many different ethnic backgrounds, languages, views, and opinions. Only through you and the salvation given through Christ Jesus do we find oneness of purpose, spirit, and hope. Thank you for being God and Father of all, who is over all and through all and in all. Amen

329

This I recall to my mind, therefore have I hope. (Lamentations 3:21 KJV)

God of Love, you are continually providing for, protecting, and blessing your people, but how quickly we forget. LORD God you have opened doors we thought shut, healed when we were deathly ill, brought us up out of the muck and mire of this world we had been stuck in. LORD, let us not forget all you have done in our lives. Help us LORD to remember your continued grace, goodness, and mercy. This today is our prayer in Jesus's name. Amen

330

Humble yourselves in the sight of the Lord, and He will lift you up. (James 4:10 NKJV)

Lord God, we children of men all want to look good in front of one another. This is an act of pride not humility. Lord Jesus, help us to be humble in heart as you are humble. Lord, help us seek you with that humble heart so that one day we will be lifted–up into your eternal Glory forever. Father, we pray this in Jesus's name. Amen

331

But He was in the stern, asleep on a pillow. And they awoke Him and said to Him, "Teacher, do You not care that we are perishing?" (Mark 4:38 NKJV)

Lord Jesus, in this life we experience many storms. There are daily turbulent relationships and interactions with family, friends, acquaintances, coworkers, and total strangers. Lord Jesus, help us look to you in those situations so we may hear you say, "Peace be still", to calm the storms of our lives. Amen

332

For all the law is fulfilled in one word, *even* in this: *"You shall love your neighbor as yourself."* (Galatians 5:14 NKJV)

Lord God Almighty, we come to you in the name of Jesus asking that the light and love of Christ Jesus radiate from us as we encounter people in our daily walk. Lord God Almighty, let us introduce each person we meet to Christ the Lord and Savior of mankind. Lord accept this as our sincere act of love for each other. Lord in your mercy, hear our prayer. Amen

333

"I, even I, am he who blots out your transgressions, for my own sake, and remembers your sins no more. (Isaiah 43:25 NIV)

Gracious LORD, because of the precious blood of Jesus you blot out our confessed sins never to be remembered forevermore. We thank you in Jesus's name. Amen

334

Let us not become weary in doing good, for at the proper time we will reap a harvest if we do not give up. (Galatians 6:9 NIV)

Heavenly Father God, day after day we meticulously seek to do what is right according to your will, and day after day we fail. Father God, we know right from wrong but even when we set out to do what is right, wrong seems to prevail. Still we keep on trying; not giving up. Help us LORD God to not become discouraged but to continue to seek the better way regardless of failure so that one day we will reap the harvest of hearing Christ Jesus say, "Well done my good and faithful servant, well done". In Jesus's name we pray. Amen

335

You, therefore, have no excuse, you who pass judgment on someone else, for at whatever point you judge the other, you are condemning yourself, because you who pass judgment do the same things. (Romans 2:1 NIV)

Lord God of tolerance, patience, and kindness–we come to you in the name of Jesus. We your handmade servants judge one another without hesitation. As we judge help us to understand that we too do the very thing we judge others of doing. Lord God help us look to you the righteous judge of mankind. Father we experience your kindness towards us–which then enables us all to grow repentant hearts which brings us into right relationship with you. This helps us not judge our brothers and sisters. This is our prayer in Jesus's name. Amen

336

They grumbled in their tents and did not obey the LORD. (Psalm 106:25 NIV)

Lord Jesus, we are a grumbling people. We grumble because of prices, lines we consider too long, things which impede our haste, the work we must complete and people who do not agree with our agenda's. Lord, we grumble, murmur, and complain. Lord Jesus you died for us without murmuring, complaining, or grumbling. Help us Lord Jesus to cultivate the same attitude that is in you into ourselves that we may glorify you and not ourselves. Amen

337

The unfolding of your words gives light; it gives understanding to the simple. (Psalm 119:130 NIV)

Lord God Almighty, as we your children begin to diligently seek your word, it speaks to our spirits. Lord we begin to see the word unfold in our lives as that life-giving word which changes lives. Lord we are plain people, but your word gives us understanding. Thank you in Jesus's name. Amen

338

I have set you an example that you should do as I have done for you. (John 13:15 NIV)

Lord Jesus we live in a me, me, me society. In this world each person thinks and says it is all about me. Lord Jesus you have set us an example of serving one another as you came not to be served but to serve. Lord you know serving can be thankless, painful, and costly. Help us to serve as you served; let us do it for you. Let us seek the strength you give us that we may be able to serve others. Amen

339

And He took bread, gave thanks and broke *it*, and gave *it* to them, saying, "This is My body which is given for you; do this in remembrance of Me." (Luke 22:19 NKJV)

Lord Jesus we humbly come to you thinking of the brokenness of this world. Lord Jesus, we are a broken people living in a broken world carrying out broken relationships which have broken outcomes. Thank you, Jesus that you allowed your body to be offered as a sacrifice to appease our brokenness. Thank you, Lord Jesus that you carried our brokenness to the cross then allowed it to be buried in the grave so that one day we will be made whole when we come into your kingdom. Amen

340

My feet have closely followed his steps; I have kept to his way without turning aside. (Job 23:11 NIV)

Lord God Almighty, we humbly approach you in the name of Jesus. O God it is difficult to follow on the path set before us, yet we try. Stumbling is constant, correction is indispensable. We know O God it is the sin which lives in us which causes this reeling from inappropriate action back to correct action. Forgive our stumbling steps as we turn aside to right ourselves for Jesus's sake. In Jesus's name we pray. Amen

341

Show me your ways, O LORD, teach me your paths;(Psalm 25:4 NIV)

Lord Jesus, teach us your ways so we can then act like you and follow the path you have set before us. This is our prayer. Amen

342

Since we have now been justified by his blood, how much more shall we be saved from God's wrath through him! (Romans 5:9 NIV)

Lord Jesus, through your blood we now are justified and saved from the wrath of God. You alone are our Lord, Our God, and our salvation. Thank you. Amen

343

But love your enemies, do good to them, and lend to them without expecting to get anything back. Then your reward will be great, and you will be sons of the Most High, because he is kind to the ungrateful and wicked. (Luke 6:35 NIV)

Lord Jesus, we seek to do good in your name. Lord, give us the opportunity today to see your hand guiding us to acts of kindness towards people around our areas of operation, this–and every other day. Lord Jesus, let us do this good to bring glory to God the Father as we go in your name. Help us to remember that it is not the what, but the why, as we spread your love throughout the earth. Amen

344

You shall be holy to me; for I the LORD am holy, and I have separated you from the other peoples to be mine. (Leviticus 20:26 NRSV)

Father God in Heaven, you have set us apart that we through Christ Jesus may become dedicated to you as we place our faith in him alone. Thank you, Father God for the special gift of being your very own. Help us honor you through what we practice in our daily lives. This is our prayer, in Jesus's Holy and precious name. Amen

345

The LORD has appeared of old to me, *saying:* "Yes, I have loved you with an everlasting love; Therefore with lovingkindness I have drawn you. (Jeremiah 31:3 NKJV)

Lord Jesus, we know that despite of ethnic origin, creed, education, economic status, or gender, you love us with a love that carried you to die on Calvary's cross for all mankind. Lord Jesus, you rose again so one day we may come into your kingdom as we too shall rise to share glory with you. We love you Lord and thank you. Your everlasting love will guide us into eternity as you call us yours. Amen

346

He who pursues righteousness and love finds life, prosperity and honor. (Proverbs 21:21 NIV)

Lord God Heavenly Father help your children pursue righteousness and kindness so we may have peace on earth while we are yet on this side of eternity. This is our prayer in Jesus's precious name. Amen

347

Then he called the crowd to him along with his disciples and said: "If anyone would come after me, he must deny himself and take up his cross and follow me. (Mark 8:34 NIV)

Lord Jesus our Redeemer and God–give us the strength to lay aside our personal desires–and follow you with determination as we conform to your commands. Help us to pursue you Lord. Amen

348

Who can say, I have made my heart clean, I am pure from my sin? (Proverbs 20:9 KJV)

Father God, as we your children live in this world, we experience many things which tempt us to sin. Father God we try to keep our hearts pure, but sin is right there seeking to contaminate us. Under our own authority none of us can say I am clean. Thank you, Father God that Christ Jesus came and through him we are found clean in your sight. In Jesus's name we offer our heartfelt thanks. Amen

349

Blessed *is* the man Who walks not in the counsel of the ungodly, Nor stands in the path of sinners, Nor sits in the seat of the scornful; But his delight *is* in the law of the LORD, And in His law he meditates day and night. (Psalm 1:1-2 NKJV)

Lord Jesus, we are challenged daily by other human beings wishing to impart their agenda upon us. Lord, give us discerning hearts to know whether to turn away or accept what is shared. Lord Jesus, we do not want to be counseled by the wicked but only by your true word. Lord, in your mercy hear our prayer. Amen

350

Vindicate me, O LORD, For I have walked in my integrity. I have also trusted in the LORD; I shall not slip. Examine me, O LORD, and prove me; Try my mind and my heart. For Your lovingkindness *is* before my eyes, And I have walked in Your truth. (Psalm 26:1-3 NKJV)

Lord God Heavenly Father, we make every effort to walk in integrity without wavering. Test our hearts O God and if there be anything not pleasing to you remove it and fill that void with the Holy Spirit. LORD, hear our prayer we ask in Jesus's name. Amen

351

Commit to the LORD whatever you do, and your plans will succeed. (Proverbs 16:3 NIV)

LORD God our Father we approach your throne of Grace in the name of Jesus. Many are the plans of mankind. We often seek your presence in our attempts to accomplish a goal. Right or wrong, good, or bad we want you on our side. Perhaps LORD God the question we should ask is "whether we are on your side". Speak to our hearts Holy Spirit with direction. This is our prayer. In Jesus's name we pray. Amen

352

And we know that all things work together for good to them that love God, to them who are the called according to *his* purpose. (Romans 8:28 KJV)

Lord God in Heaven, we often encounter tribulation as we pass through this life. Lord, regardless of the trials and troubles life hands us, we know you are allowing certain events and have already ordained the outcome. We love you Lord. We praise you Lord. We thank you for doing for us what we could never do for ourselves. Lord, even when it does not look like what we think it should, we know you are in control and our best interest is your desired outcome. We ask you to hear our prayer in Jesus's name. Amen

353

So then faith *comes* by hearing, and hearing by the word of God. (Romans 10:17 NKJV)

Dear Lord, help us to seek you through your word so that our faith increase. Let us hear your word as it is sung, prayed, and preached. We pray this in Jesus's name. Amen

354

The LORD your God in your midst, The Mighty One, will save; He will rejoice over you with gladness, He will quiet *you* with His love, He will rejoice over you with singing." (Zephaniah 3:17 NKJV)

O Lord our God, you dwell among us constantly, saving us from unseen hazards. O God you have made us your delight and your love gives us peace and comfort. Because of you O God we have a heart full of singing and joy. Lord hear our prayer in Jesus's name. Amen

355

"This, then, is how you should pray: "'Our Father in heaven, hallowed be your name, (Matthew 6:9 NIV)

Dear Father in Heaven, we your children thank you that you think so highly of us despite our often-wayward activities. Only you are wholly, Holy. Thank you for loving us so. In Jesus's precious name we pray. Amen

356

Give us this day our daily bread. (Matthew 6:11 KJV)

Father God hear us as we ask with open hand for a daily portion of the bounty of this earth. LORD in the context of bread it could be defined as our job or the funds we reap from offering our lives towards work. LORD, give us enough to sustain us and sometimes we ask for enough to share so that all are filled. We pray this prayer in Jesus's name. Amen

357

Thy kingdom come. Thy will be done in earth, as *it is* in heaven. (Matthew 6:10 KJV)

Lord God Heavenly Father, we come in the name of Jesus asking that your will be done here on earth until the return of our Lord and Savior Jesus Christ. Father you will give perfect harmony among your people. Nothing better can be given in this world of darkness. Lord in your mercy hear our prayer. Lord we individually ask, "Let you will on earth begin with me". Amen

358

This *is* the day the LORD has made; We will rejoice and be glad in it. (Psalm 118:24 NKJV)

LORD God Heavenly Father, we approach you in the name of Jesus asking that by the power of your Holy Spirit help us to maximize this day and give you glory through our efforts. This is our prayer in Jesus's name. Amen

359

Set your mind on things above, not on things on the earth. (Colossians 3:2 NKJV)

LORD God Almighty, we your hand made servants are presented daily with circumstances which can either give joy or disappoint. Help us LORD God, to keep our hearts focused on Christ, more than everything else. We want our significance and validation to come from Christ Jesus and all else to remain secondary in our lives. Lord help us to focus on the heavenly realm where Christ awaits us with life, not the earthly realm where we are dying. This is our prayer as we pray in Jesus's name. Amen

360

"But I say to you who hear: Love your enemies, do good to those who hate you, bless those who curse you, and pray for those who spitefully use you. (Luke 6:27-28 NKJV)

Lord Jesus, you are the epitome of true love. Lord, you have directed us to love our enemies and do good to those who hate us. Lord you say bless those who curse us and Lord you say pray for those who abuse us. Lord, in and of our own strength we cannot do this, but through you Lord Jesus we can do all things. Lord, strengthen us to accomplish your will and bring glory to God our Father. Amen

361

For You, O God, have tested us; You have refined us as silver is refined. (Psalm 66:10 NKJV)

LORD God Heavenly Father, you allow us your children to pass through the crucible of trials that we may be refined into the Disciples of Christ who can best serve mankind. Father God although the refining is not pleasant, the result brings you glory. Help us not reject the process, that we may shine like pure silver and gold. We pray in Jesus's name. Amen

362

for it is God who works in you both to will and to do for *His* good pleasure. (Philippians 2:13 NKJV)

Lord it is through you that we can do your will and accomplish what is pleasing to you. Thank you for empowerment and purpose. Amen

363

Let us therefore come boldly unto the throne of grace, that we may obtain mercy, and find grace to help in time of need. (Hebrews 4:16 KJV)

Lord God, through Christ Jesus you have given us approval to approach your throne of Grace as we seek help in our time of need. Thank you, Lord God Heavenly Father. Amen

364

Remain in me, and I will remain in you. No branch can bear fruit by itself; it must remain in the vine. Neither can you bear fruit unless you remain in me. (John 15:4 NIV)

Lord Jesus your word says if we abide in you, we can bear much fruit. Lord help us abide in you in all matters of life towards self and others. This is our prayer. Amen

365

A fool's mouth is his undoing, and his lips are a snare to his soul. (Proverbs 18:7 NIV)

Lord, help us keep our words sweet because we may one day have to eat them. Lord, keep our mouths from speaking trouble into the lives of ourselves and others. This we pray in Jesus's name. Amen

366

But thanks be to God, who gives us the victory through our Lord Jesus Christ. (1 Corinthians 15:57 NRSV)

LORD God, our Father in Heaven help us your hand made servants to always humbly stand viewing the blood soaked cross of Christ Jesus. Help us Father God to remember the debt that Christ paid on our behalf to redeem us. Help us LORD God to have a willingness to release others from the debts they owe us for the harm they have caused. Help us LORD to do what we cannot do alone. This is our Prayer and through Christ Jesus we pray it. Amen

367

For the great day of His wrath has come, and who is able to stand?" (Revelation 6:17 NKJV)

Lord Jesus, the day of your return is closer today than it was yesterday. Lord, even in our best efforts we fall short and go astray. Thank you, for your blood Lord which offers us Grace and Mercy which cleans us up, many of us know in our hearts we above all others need it. Amen

368

If it is possible, as far as it depends on you, live at peace with everyone. (Romans 12:18 NIV)

Father God we come in the name of Jesus. Father there is much conflict happening in this world. Conflict happens in the neighborhood, at the job, in the home, in Christ's church and in in the world in general. Father God there is even conflict within our own hearts as we become divided on issues of a personal nature. Father God help us live peaceably with others and with self. This we pray in Jesus's name. Amen

369

For God has not given us a spirit of fear, but of power and of love and of a sound mind. (2 Timothy 1:7 NKJV)

Lord Jesus, we need peace in this world. Lord Jesus, empower us with the character to resolve conflict, so there be peace on earth and goodwill towards one another. Let us not be afraid to stand before mankind with words of love which usher in harmony in this world. Amen

370

Do not fear, for I am with you; I will bring your offspring from the east, and from the west I will gather you; (Isaiah 43:5 NRSV)

Gracious Lord, you protect our coming and going therefore we need fear nothing inaugurated by evil. Lord you alone are our Savior and you bring us back from remote places into your presence along with the body of believers. Because of you we are no longer isolated. Thank you, Lord Jesus for being with us. Amen

371

This is the day the LORD has made; let us rejoice and be glad in it. (Psalm 118:24 NIV)

Thank You, Lord for this new day which is filled with new opportunities. Lord we cannot navigate this day alone, so we ask that you hear us as we call upon you each step of the way. There will be things we cannot anticipate and things we are not prepared for, but you know all things because you know the end before the beginning. We thank you Lord for the gift of a new day; we rejoice and are certainly are glad. We pray in Jesus's name. Amen

372

He that spared not his own Son, but delivered him up for us all, how shall he not with him also freely give us all things? (Romans 8:32 KJV)

LORD God our Heavenly Father, we know that because you did not withhold from us Salvation. LORD, by offering up Jesus your only begotten son as our propitiation to you we know you will withhold no good thing from us. We thank you in Jesus's name. Amen

373

"Let not your heart be troubled; you believe in God, believe also in Me. (John 14:1 NKJV)

LORD God Our Father, as we trust in you help us to trust in Christ our Savior. He has prepared a place for us so one day we will be with Him. LORD, help those who still do not believe—to come to the knowledge of the truth that through Christ alone we will be saved. LORD, this is our prayer as we pray in Jesus's name. Amen

374

Your ears shall hear a word behind you, saying, "This *is* the way, walk in it," Whenever you turn to the right hand Or whenever you turn to the left. (Isaiah 30:21 NKJV)

O Lord our God, you have given us a new day; we thank you. Now Lord we ask for a fresh new word to guide us through the situations we find ourselves in this day. Help our ears and hearts to be attuned to your word as that word guide us along our way. This we pray in the name of the Father, Son and Holy Spirit. Amen

375

"For you shall go out with joy, And be led out with peace; The mountains and the hills Shall break forth into singing before you, And all the trees of the field shall clap *their* hands. (Isaiah 55:12 NKJV)

LORD God Heavenly Father, we come in the name of Jesus acknowledging your eternal goodness. LORD, even now nature breaks forth in a chorus as the birds of the air sing songs of thanksgiving and the leaves of the trees clap their appreciation for you. LORD, the plants of the earth sway with dance as your spirit passes by. And LORD our human hearts flutter at the thought of who you are as our eyes fill with tears of joy. Thank you, God. In Jesus's name we pray. Amen

380

However, when He, the Spirit of truth, has come, He will guide you into all truth; for He will not speak on His own *authority,* but whatever He hears He will speak; and He will tell you things to come. (John 16:13 NKJV)

LORD God, it is astounding that we often listen to the voices of other human beings with full acceptance of their statements as fact. Lord there are those who question the validity of the scriptures. LORD, only the Spirit of Truth can guide us into all truth which comes from your scriptures. Help us to become sensitive as he declares to us things which are to come so we are prepared for the coming of our Lord and Savior Jesus Christ. This is our prayer, in Jesus's name. Amen

381

and to clothe yourselves with the new self, created according to the likeness of God in true righteousness and holiness. (Ephesians 4:24 NRSV)

LORD God Almighty, we, each one of your hand made servants have a new self within, just waiting to emerge. Christ has produced in each believer the desire to be more Christ like in all we say, think and do. O God help our new self to materialize daily then after the metamorphosis we glorify you as the world views you in us. This we pray in the name of the Father, Son and Holy Spirit. Amen

382

When Jesus reached the spot, he looked up and said to him, "Zacchaeus, come down immediately. I must stay at your house today." (Luke 19:5 NIV)

Lord Jesus, please dwell with us individually and collectively today and every day. Lord in your mercy, hear our prayer. Amen

383

I will cry out to God Most High, To God who performs *all things* for me. (Psalm 57:2 NKJV)

Lord God, through us you fulfill your purposes. Lord, as an instrument in the hands of a master musician produces music which moves the heart and invokes emotion within your people. We ask that you the master of our universe use us in such a way as to demonstrate the value of an instrument in the hands of the master. This we pray in Jesus's name. Amen

384

But seek ye first the kingdom of God, and his righteousness; and all these things shall be added unto you. (Matthew 6:33 KJV)

Lord Jesus, people try to go through life doing things in their own way, they soon encounter difficulties beyond their control because Kingdom direction was omitted. Within we know we must first seek your kingdom then all else is added. Help us to begin with the basics in all things. Help us seek first your Kingdom with its divine principles as we pursue the activities associated with life. This is our prayer in your name. Amen

385

But the Lord answered her, "Martha, Martha, you are worried and distracted by many things; there is need of only one thing. Mary has chosen the better part, which will not be taken away from her." (Luke 10:41-42 NRSV)

Lord Jesus, as we go about the business of daily life, we encounter many voices. Some voices will encourage, direct, suggest, offend, teach, or rebuke. Lord we will encounter situations which call for our attention or so we think. Lord we want to filter out those other voices and extraneous activities and hear you alone. Please make that happen as we desire to hear and follow you, and you alone. Lord in your mercy, hear our prayer. Amen

386

Who *is* a God like You, Pardoning iniquity And passing over the transgression of the remnant of His heritage? He does not retain His anger forever, Because He delights *in* mercy. (Micah 7:18 NKJV)

We thank you LORD God Almighty for forgiving us through Christ our Savior. No longer do you see us as sinful people but people who place our faith in Christ Jesus. Father you now see us through the purifying blood of your precious Lamb who was the sacrifice for the sins of the world. Thank you for your mercy won for us by the blood. Amen

387

'Call to Me, and I will answer you, and show you great and mighty things, which you do not know.' (Jeremiah 33:3 NKJV)

LORD God, you are the great promise keeper. We call upon you this day and every day as we await your proclamation of the deep unsearchable things that only you know and share with us. Because you are our God we are assured of your response. We thank you in Jesus's name. Amen

388

the voice of joy and the voice of gladness, the voice of the bridegroom and the voice of the bride, the voice of those who will say: "Praise the LORD of hosts, For the LORD *is* good, For His mercy *endures* forever"-- *and* of those *who will* bring the sacrifice of praise into the house of the LORD. For I will cause the captives of the land to return as at the first,' says the LORD. (Jeremiah 33:11 NKJV)

Heavenly Father, through your continued mercy which is found in Christ you give our voices joy. We praise you Lord; your mercy endures forever. Amen

389

**A merry heart makes a cheerful countenance,
But by sorrow of the heart the spirit is broken.
(Proverbs 15:13 NKJV)**

Lord God Heavenly Father, as we walk this earth, we see the faces of those around us. Lord, there are faces of joy and faces of sadness. As we think of your goodness which is demonstrated through Christ Jesus, we can have faces which express joy and our hearts are happy. We offer you our gratitude and praise in Jesus's name. Amen

390

He who listens to a life-giving rebuke will be at home among the wise. (Proverbs 15:31 NIV)

Lord Jesus your Word up lifts encourages and rebukes. Lord, give us ears to hear and hearts to accept the life-giving rebuke found in your Word that we may one day dwell among the wise. Amen

Conversing With God

Scripture Reference

Genesis 10, 14, 158, 219, 315,

Exodus 53, 69, 88,

Leviticus 344,

Numbers 72,

Deuteronomy 73, 138, 163, 206, 212, 232,

Joshua

Judges

Ruth

1 Samuel 82, 125, 248

2 Samuel

1 Kings 76,

2 Kings 113,

1Chronicles 191, 223,

2 Chronicles

Ezra 214,

Nehemiah

Ester

Job 8, 322, 340,

Psalms 6, 17, 18, 25, 26, 46, 51, 54, 56, 61, 64, 68, 75, 89, 92, 102, 103, 116, 118, 120, 128, 129, 130, 133, 134, 142, 150, 155, 162, 164, 166, 174, 176, 178, 179, 181, 182, 186, 189, 195, 204, 209, 210, 216, 218, 220, 227, 231, 233, 246, 257, 262, 275, 283, 285, 294, 296, 299, 302, 305, 310, 317, 326, 336, 337, 341, 349, 350, 358, 361, 371, 383

Proverbs 27, 45, 62, 74, 105, 117, 135, 144, 161, 168, 211, 241, 254, 261, 264, 291, 325, 346, 348, 351, 365, 389, 390

Ecclesiastes 243, 259, 287, 288, 304

Song of Songs

Isaiah 40, 48, 55, 63, 80, 81, 91, 96, 111, 127, 167, 249, 263, 265, 311, 333, 370, 374, 375,

Jeremiah 21, 39, 67, 229, 230, 238, 345, 387, 388

Lamentations 60, 329,

Ezekiel

Daniel

Hosea

Joel 28,

Amos

Obadiah

Jonah

Micah 225, 386

Nahum 1

Habakkuk 93, 236

Zephaniah 237, 354,

Haggai

Zechariah 245,

Malachi 58, 226,

Matthew 5, 15, 30, 65, 83, 101, 146, 207, 208, 224, 242, 252, 267, 286, 303, 324, 355, 356, 357, 384

Mark 84, 327, 331, 347,

Luke 24, 201, 203, 274, 279, 295, 300, 306, 339, 343, 360, 382, 385

John 12, 47, 104, 114, 139, 140, 187, 193, 197, 251, 276, 284, 289, 293, 338, 364, 373, 380,

Acts 97, 119, 184, 202, 278, 281

Romans 2, 3, 23, 43, 57, 70, 71, 77, 132, 148, 151, 170,180, 183, 213, 239, 240, 247, 253, 255, 258, 266, 280, 282, 313, 335, 342, 352, 353, 368, 372,

1 Corinthians 9, 29, 66, 78, 106, 123, 124, 126, 141, 194, 196, 205, 234, 298, 366,

2 Corinthians 49, 87, 99, 109, 110, 152, 153, 157, 159, 173, 228

Galatians 137, 221, 244, 320, 332, 334,

Ephesians 13, 50, 52, 122, 147, 175, 250, 277, 328, 381,

Philippians 11, 90, 98, 115, 149, 171, 190, 270, 290,297, 312, 362,

Colossians 19, 42, 44, 86, 112, 154, 269, 271, 307, 359,

1 Thessalonians 41, 268

2 Thessalonians

1 Timothy 308, 318,

2 Timothy 369,

Titus 16, 107, 156, 314,

Philemon

Hebrews 59, 94, 100, 108, 121, 177, 185, 198, 199, 222, 301, 303, 309, 316, 363,

James 79, 136, 192, 260, 302, 321, 330,

1 Peter 4, 7, 95, 143, 160, 215, 235, 272,

2 Peter 131,

1 John 20, 22, 85, 145, 169, 200, 217, 256, 273, 319, 323,

2 John

3 John

Jude

Revelation 165, 172, 188, 292, 367,